FEAR NO EVIL

*Tackling Quarterbacks and Demons on
My Way to the Hall of Fame*

CHARLES HALEY

with Jeff Sullivan

TRIUMPH
BOOKS

Library of Congress Cataloging-in-Publication Data

Names: Haley, Charles, author. | Sullivan, Jeff, author.

Title: Fear no evil : tackling quarterbacks and demons on my way to the Hall of Fame / Charles Haley with Jeff Sullivan.

Description: Chicago, Illinois : Triumph Books, LLC, [2016] | Includes bibliographical references and index.

Identifiers: LCCN 2016013156 | ISBN 9781629372594 (alk. paper)

Subjects: LCSH: Haley, Charles | Football players—United States—Biography.

Classification: LCC GV939.H265 A3 2016 | DDC 796.332092 [B]—dc23 LC record available at https://lccn.loc.gov/2016013156

This book is available in quantity at special discounts for your group or organization. For further information, contact:

Triumph Books LLC
814 North Franklin Street
Chicago, Illinois 60610
(312) 337-0747
www.triumphbooks.com

Printed in U.S.A.

ISBN: 978-1-62937-259-4

Design by Amy Carter

For my four children, Princess, Charles Jr., Brianna, and Madison, whom I love unconditionally and have seen me at my worst. They have been my inspiration to become a better man and father.

Yea, though I walk through the valley of the shadow of death,
I will fear no evil...

—Psalm 23:4

Contents

Foreword *by Ronnie Lott* 9

Foreword *by Jerry Jones* 15

Introduction 21

1. The Truth and Fiction of the Locker Room Stories 27

2. Growing Up in Gladys 43

3. Opportunity of a Lifetime 61

4. Welcome to the NFL 77

5. Self-Destruction 97

6. Moving to Big D 117

7. Going Back-to-Back with the 'Boys 135

8. Triumph and Tragedy 151

9. Back in San Fran 165

10. Pain and Gain 171

11. Living Bipolar 183

12. Hall of Fame Induction 205

13. Reflection 221

Acknowledgments 233

Foreword

IT DIDN'T TAKE LONG for me to form my first impression of Charles Haley. Even when he was a rookie with the San Francisco 49ers in 1986, it was obvious that, while he didn't have all the understanding he would need to become a top-tier defensive end, he possessed the deepest desire to succeed. He was one of those rare teammates, one of those rare people you come across in this world, who was willing to work until he couldn't and was willing to maximize his body for the sole objective of winning.

Here's a kid from James Madison University, certainly not a big-time college football program, and he's supposed to replace one of the greatest defensive ends to ever play the game in Fred Dean. It didn't take long, though, to see that Charles would be able to fill those shoes. We were incredibly fortunate to replace one Pro Football Hall of Famer with another. That doesn't happen often.

A lot of guys come and go in the NFL and never grasp the opportunity. They are sitting around right now wondering why their career didn't go like they thought it would. It's because they weren't committed like Charles was. Every day Charles showed up with the knowledge and understanding of what an honor and privilege it is to play football at that level. He invested himself fully. The man would run and run until he could run no more. The man would watch film until there was no film left. He respected what his name stood for.

Charles is always working someone. At this very moment, Charles is working an angle. He's helping someone. He's talking to some store owner about donating a bunch of bread to feed hungry children. He's making calls to find extra computers for inner-city students. He's constantly working the system to help others.

He is a lot smarter than anyone gives him credit for. Sure, as a football player, everyone understood his genius for the game, but I'm talking about off the field. He's James Bond. The man walks into a room and assesses everyone there within minutes. He knows who's scared, who's not, who leads, who needs help, who falters under pressure. He reads people better than anyone. I've mentioned this to him, and he brushes it off, saying when you grow up in a family like his you have to read people.

I know players who played for Bill Walsh a lot longer than Charles, but he understood the coach after just a few days. That's why they connected so perfectly. There were times when Charles knew some of our assistant coaches better than they knew themselves.

Charles had some issues with coaches—with authority in general—but I guarantee you this: every single coach would say, "Give me someone who plays as hard as Haley." Charles was that guy in the fourth quarter still running at first-quarter speed. That motor of his never stopped revving.

Here's what I will never, ever understand: the 49ers changed the weight of the entire league by trading Charles to the Dallas Cowboys. San Francisco would have won three more Super Bowls if it hadn't. Instead, they sent one of the game's premier pass rushers to Dallas on a singular mission of revenge.

They didn't have any perspective. It's like a family member. Sometimes you don't understand why they do what they do, but you still love them. The 49ers didn't understand why winning and teammates mattered so much to Charles. They didn't understand his level of passion. They didn't understand what resides in a man's heart when his sole purpose is to be a champion, to strive each and every day to be the best for his teammates. They didn't understand Charles, so they sent him to Dallas, and he kicked their rear end for the next five years.

Yeah, he went psycho after a loss; he was that angry, he cared that deeply. That doesn't mean he's crazy and that the team can't exist and succeed because of him. But that became the story. Charles is crazy. Tell me this, how can Charles be crazy if he knew the assignments for every single one of his teammates on every single play? Charles was the smartest guy on the field.

I'm not saying Charles was always easy in the locker room. He was cool with me because we were friends. He knew I looked out for him. But this one time, Charles had Jerry Rice in a headlock after practice and he wouldn't let go unless Rice said "uncle." You're talking about two of the all-time competitors. Rice obviously has no chance against Charles, but he's not giving in and he more or less passes out. Charles walks away, and we're all thinking that this really awkward moment is over. Then less than a minute later, Jerry is chasing Charles around the locker room with a fire extinguisher. That was one of the funniest things I've ever seen.

Charles couldn't be in a better place right now. It's tough not knowing where to go in life. From high school and college to then the NFL, football was his whole world. There's a little time for family, but for 20 years or so, it's football. Then what? You have to relearn how to live, how to exist and flourish in a new environment. I struggled with this—a lot of us do—and Charles definitely did. It's just unfortunate that we have to live our lives out in public.

A lot of that adjustment is by experiment. Charles tried coaching for a few years and realized that wasn't his thing—at least on a full-time basis. Instead, he decided he wanted to help people, and I couldn't be more proud of him. More than anyone, Charles understands his purpose in this world. Charles is always a phone call away. How can you not love that this tough-guy Hall of Famer who spends every day of his life now trying to help people? What an asset to society he is. Just like on the football field, Charles is giving the kind of effort that less than 1 percent of people give to any endeavor their entire lives.

Charles was a gift to the game of football. The kind of dedication and passion he brought, you just don't see that today. There was no greater honor during my career than calling Charles Haley a teammate. And it will be my honor every day for the remainder of our lives to call him my beloved friend.

—*Ronnie Lott*

Foreword

WHEN THE DALLAS COWBOYS reported to training camp in 1992, we were on the cusp of greatness. Our offense was already loaded with big-time playmakers, dynamic leadership, and, of course, the Triplets—Troy Aikman, Emmitt Smith, and Michael Irvin. Still, there was something missing. Someone, really, and that someone was Charles Haley.

Charles was the final piece of the puzzle. Those three championship Cowboys teams don't win the Super Bowl without Charles Haley. We weren't complete until he arrived. We went from a pretty good football team to one of the greatest dynasties the game has ever witnessed, and really the only difference between the two was Charles.

The season before Charles arrived, we won 11 games and another in the playoffs, but we weren't good enough to win it all for one simple reason: we didn't have a pass rush. Only two teams finished the 1991 season with fewer sacks. The next Super Bowl champion that doesn't have a formidable pass rush will be the first.

So when the San Francisco 49ers called about trading a couple of draft picks for one of the premier pass rushers in the NFL, we were definitely suspicious. Both of us felt like we would be competing for conference supremacy over the next three or four years, and yet they wanted to send us one of their best players. This just doesn't happen. This is like a fellow oilman calling me back in the day and saying, "Jerry, I have this well that just keeps gushing oil, but I don't want it any longer. You interested?"

Damn right, we were interested. So I called 49ers owner Eddie DeBartolo Jr. back and said, "What's the deal? Why are you guys willing to trade Charles to a rival team—to anyone for that matter?"

And he was honest with me. He told me everything Charles had done and that George Seifert and his coaches had decided that they'd just had enough. Again, he told me *everything*, every story, every incident. When he finished, I said, "Is that all? We can make that work. Let's do the deal." Later that night my good friend, the late, great Al Davis, owner of the then–Los Angeles Raiders, called me and said, "Congratulations. You just won the Super Bowl."

The following day, when Charles arrived in Dallas, I was there to drive him back to the team offices. I wanted to talk with him, let him know who I was, what I was about, and that I didn't want him to change. I just wanted him to be Charles, do his thing, play some ball, and help us win some Super Bowls. I also promised him that, no matter what, I would have his back. I was 100 percent committed to Charles. It was important for him to know, to understand, that I wasn't trying to change him or anything of the sort. I also told him, "We will be Super Bowl champions. Not down the road. We start today. You're the final piece."

He certainly was. We nearly doubled our sacks his first year, led the league in total defense, and won the Super Bowl. We won another one the following season and a third in 1995. We became the first team in NFL history to win three Lombardi Trophies in four years. Charles was the difference maker for us in doing that. He brought a personal spirit and competitive drive to our organization that changed the course of Cowboys history.

I remember when we went to the White House after winning that first title, and Bill Clinton was president. He's shaking hands with all of us, and I see Charles lean down and whisper something to him. Bill kind of chuckled. I'm not going to repeat what he said, but let's just say it was classic Charles. It didn't matter whose company he was in. Charles was always going to be Charles.

There are a lot of misconceptions about Charles. First, he was one of the smartest players I've ever been around. We would talk football all the time. Charles wasn't always the easiest guy to communicate with if the topic was anything besides football, but he could talk football for hours. He was in many ways the quarterback of the defense, which is unheard of for a pass rusher.

They always talk about sacks, too, but here's what needs to be said about Charles. The guys around him racked up a whole bunch of sacks because the other team was so focused on stopping Charles with two and three blockers.

Charles was old-school tough, where his will and determination would just overcome whatever injury he was dealing with. Those first four years he was here, Charles was probably on the injury report just about every week, but he missed just six games. He did that for the fans, he did that for his teammates, he did that for the Dallas Cowboys. He didn't want to let any of us down. Even those who may not have adored him did respect him, I can promise you that.

There is no way of minimalizing the importance of accountability with any team—sports or otherwise—a business team, a sales team. And Charles held his teammates accountable. He said the things that were uncomfortable for others to broach, and that went a long way toward our success.

Some were surprised when I inducted Charles into the Ring of Honor in 2011 since he only played five seasons in Dallas. First, there is nothing I take more seriously than who we include in this prestigious group of men who have represented America's Team. That's why there are only 21 who have been so honored. For me, though, it was one of those absolutely, positively, let's-do-this kinds of decisions. This franchise has won five Super Bowls, and for three of them, Charles was an important anchor.

You will never see me in the vicinity of Charles without a smile on my face, probably laughing at his impersonation of me. He's been doing his Jerry for a long time now, and it's actually not bad. I'd be walking into the locker room, coming around that corner, and I'd hear Charles doing me with everyone laughing. Then he'd look up and see me, and everyone would fall silent, but I would just give him a smile.

Just like I promised, Charles always knew I had his back. And nothing was more important to Charles. I'm not sure how many people understood that. Charles always felt like everyone was coming after him, was out to get him. He just needed to know who he could trust. And once he trusted you, no one was more loyal than Charles.

The man Charles has become these last few years—the way he has so honestly and genuinely dealt with his bipolar disorder, how he has reached out to so many current players about his own issues, how deeply he cares about helping others—is impressive. There is so much to take, so many valuable life lessons to learn from his story.

Through his ups and downs, Charles always has been an incredibly loving father to his four children, and they have done so well for themselves. The three oldest are college graduates, and the fourth is going to Stanford on a soccer scholarship. Charles has a lot to be proud of.

And I couldn't be more proud of Charles. For so many reasons, he's one of my favorite players. I adore him so much.

—*Jerry Jones*

Introduction

THERE ARE A LOT OF FOLKS who seem to think they know who I am. Not only the football player I was, but also the man. That's interesting because for the majority of my career, I didn't know who I was. And to be honest, that's been a daily struggle all my life.

There are good days and bad, like most of us, I'm guessing. It's been better since I was diagnosed with bipolar disorder in 2003. Well, to be honest, a lot of folks had me diagnosed long before then, but that was when I finally accepted the reality of my situation, and I've been taking my medication since.

There are still ups and downs, and when I'm down, that can be pretty tough. It seems like it's mostly at night, when I'm alone and feeling worthless. I've been in those real, real dark places where I thought about killing myself. I had something I could be really good at with football, but then when that's gone, it's hard to find yourself. So I went to those terribly dark places in my mind. What kept me from killing myself is that I realized I couldn't have a relationship with Jesus Christ if I committed suicide. That always brought my head up.

I go to a psychiatrist and a counselor now. I sit down and I'm open and honest. Holding it in, that's what I did my whole life. I internalized everything somebody said, everything somebody did, and then guess what? I couldn't let it go.

I always sensed that somebody was going to attack me, so I attacked first. One of the best moments of my life—this was five years ago or so—I was talking to Emmitt Smith, the all-time leading rusher in NFL history and my former teammate with the Dallas Cowboys. He said something and I just started to attack him. And he says, "Charles, you won't let anyone be your friend."

I walked away and I thought about that. He was right. When I got around guys, I might say one, two things, and then—boom—the pit bull came out. I appreciated Emmitt helping me understand what I was doing. I'm sure a lot of my former teammates wish I had figured that out about 20 years earlier. The worst part of being bipolar is that I've scared my family, my ex-wife Karen, and my four kids because of the hopelessness and worthlessness that I felt. Even though I've done so many great things, I couldn't see it, and that's when I knew that something was wrong.

You know, a lot of people have depression and don't have an outlet. Playing football, watching film, just being around my teammates—even if I didn't feel like talking with them that particular day—that was my outlet. There were days I would wake up and just want to stay there in my bed or on the couch watching cartoons and pretend the world didn't exist. That's how depression works. During the season, however, at least I had football. That would get me up and dressed and out the door. Without football, there's no telling where my life would have ended up.

Nowadays, when I start feeling depressed, I go to Starbucks, open the doors, and I buy somebody something. I try and reach out to people who know me, and we get into a conversation. They start talking about their kids, their family, and now I'm not thinking about my past or how I'm feeling. I'm thinking about how somebody else is feeling, so it takes me out of my own world.

It's tragic that the human mind can work that way. I mean, look, no one needs to tell me how fortunate I have been after coming from a childhood without indoor plumbing in Gladys, Virginia. And it's all because of football, a game I loved playing more than words can explain.

It's still hard for me to grasp the significance of me winning five Super Bowls. You hear all of this stuff about how we were only an offensive team; those teams were only winners because of the offense.

Well, on all my teams that won the Super Bowl, we were a top three defense each time. My first four years in Dallas, we were first in total defense twice and allowed the second fewest points in the conference in three of the four seasons.

It's been 20 years since I won my fifth ring. And I'm still the only player to do it. I knew going into that Super Bowl against the Pittsburgh Steelers that no one had won five because my former San Francisco 49ers teammate and good friend Ronnie Lott called me the morning of the game and told me there were a bunch of guys with four but none with five. I laughed and told him that if we did win, and I thought we would, that I was going to put all five rings on and pop him upside the head. So I got to do that, which was fun. It was more a love tap, though. I do love Ronnie.

Tom Brady seems to have the best chance to match my five. Regardless of if he does, I'm the first one to do so, and they can never take that away from me. And you know what, for me to stay relevant, maybe someone else needs to get there, to win five. If that happens, I'm not going to take anything away from that player. They will have all my respect and admiration because, if you can get to that house five times and win it, I know you deserve the honor and praise.

Heck, I want someone to break it someday and win six. It will be even more exciting if it happens soon while I'm able to enjoy it—and hopefully enjoy it with them, maybe talk about it, and tell some stories. That's going to be a pretty exclusive club. It's been lonely these last 20 years. It's no fun being on the mountaintop by yourself. You need someone to compare journeys with, see what they sacrificed to reach the top.

I have regrets, a whole bunch of regrets, about the way I treated my teammates, my coaches, my family, and people in general during my playing career, but as far as winning, as far as maximizing my team's opportunity for success, I have zero. But it required a lot of sacrifice. I sacrificed my back, my knees. I've been parking in handicapped spaces for almost 10 years now. It takes me a while to get around, and I just turned 52 this past January. I'm not exactly an old man, but let me tell you, my body is old. We won Super Bowls and we made the fans happy. I mean, when it comes to playing in the NFL, that's Mount Olympus, where the football gods reside. That's why we all play, so I'm okay with how it all turned out, and I'm paying the price with my body every waking hour.

I was willing to sacrifice it all—physically and mentally. Again, though, I have no regrets about how I pushed my teammates in terms of being better football players, in terms of caring more about winning because you know what? At the end of the day, when I walk in a room, people know I'm a winner. When a lot of other guys walk in a room, they could play 13 years, make a lot of money, but people won't know who the hell they are.

People want to be around winners. They want to be around people who know how to sacrifice. I go do a lot of charity work, autograph shows, football clinics, speeches, and people want to know about success. If they want to know about failure, there's a whole bunch of people, ex-football players included, they can ask that about stuff.

I've never been really great at expressing myself, well, at least my inner feelings. I can tell a joke. I was the class clown growing up, and that continued into the locker rooms of my high school, college, and pro teams. There are a lot of stories about me out there. Some are true, some are ridiculously exaggerated, and others are simply fiction.

There's a quote I really like, from the Greek writer Nikos Kazantzakis: "Since we cannot change reality, let us change the eyes which see reality." Deep stuff, huh? You weren't expecting that from ol' Charles were you? That's my goal with this book—at least one of them. To change the eyes with which the world sees Charles Haley. I'm also hopeful that through my journey—with bipolar disorder and depression and where I am today—that maybe my story can help someone else.

Chapter 1

The Truth and Fiction of the
Locker Room Stories

OKAY, LET'S DO THIS. I'm sure a lot of people reading this book want to know about all that crazy stuff I supposedly did—the locker room stories. I honestly don't know all of the stories out there. I don't. I know some folks are going to say I'm full of it, but I never listen to the radio, I hardly ever watch television, and I never, ever, ever read the sports section. People can say what they want, they can write what they want, and people can feel however they want to feel about me. I know the truth. I'm just a guy who lived in a frat house-like environment, which is an NFL locker room, and some former teammates—because of my actions toward them—chose to go out and tell these stories in an attempt to take me down a notch.

I didn't read that one book that basically started it all. You know what that guy's deal was? All he was doing was trying to sell copies. He didn't do any background work on any of the stories, he didn't confirm them with multiple teammates, and he certainly didn't talk to me. He didn't want to have anyone tell him anything different. That was always my biggest issue with the media in general. Even if they take the time to get both sides of the story, which they don't always do, they write whatever angle is the juiciest. What's going to sell? Charles pulling out his junk sells.

Now, that's not to say I wasn't crazy at times. I had some issues with teammates, including 49ers defensive lineman Jim Burt. We went at it a few times. There were some fisticuffs. The day before Super Bowl XXIV, we had this dinner. I was standing in the hallway outside the dining room, and he pulled my jacket up over my arms and headbutted me. He just snuck up behind me. I never heard him. He busted my lip pretty good. And when I was able to get my jacket off my face, I see a security guard standing right there. He didn't do anything. The guy just let Burt do that to me, so I was convinced I was set up. I've never spoken to Burt since, so I'm not sure what the deal was.

You know what, though? I'm a legend in people's minds. They have been embellishing other stories for a while. I wish I did half of the stuff that people say I've done. I have to tell you this, though: I had fun. The rules of engagement were, at least were supposed to be, what happens in the locker room stays in the locker room. We were supposed to be a brotherhood. That was our home. No one was supposed to be telling stories to bitch-ass writers.

I have some stories, I have some stories that would blow some minds, but I'm not sure what ratting out teammates would accomplish. I'll tell you the stuff I did, my firsthand experiences, but why sell out a former teammate? Whether you like a guy or not, we went on that field together and bled, we fought as one, and when that's over, you should have the other guy's back. So, that's what we have. We have cowards who wait until we're no longer in that locker room together and then say what they want to say with their own little twist to it.

At least a guy like Chad Hennings—my teammate with the Cowboys, a heck of a defensive tackle and a former Air Force pilot—confronted me when we were playing. I respect that, and we're friendly now. We have done prayer breakfasts together. Yeah, I pushed Chad one time at training camp. We were in a third-story hotel room, and within seconds he had me hanging out an open window. If he pushed me at that point, or hit me, I was falling out and getting seriously injured. Sometimes I just needed to be reeled in.

I'm not sure anyone possessed the ability to piss off my teammates quite like I could. At practice I was once messing with running back Emmitt Smith pretty good. And he was not enjoying it. I was hitting him after the play was called dead, I was talking trash to him, I was sneaking up behind him in the huddle and hitting him in the nuts.

Finally, Emmitt reached his breaking point and just grabbed one of my fingers and yanked. I was standing there calling him this and that and every insult you can think of, and he just pulls my ring finger out of the socket. That shit hurt. He broke it. Emmitt broke my finger, and it's still messed up to this day. Every time I see him, I remind him about it, and he just laughs and says, "Charles, you should have left me alone."

It's worth pointing out that while I was obviously unstable and dealing with some mental issues, the bipolar disorder first and foremost, my antics weren't just me being off my rocker. Some were calculated, as messed up as that may sound. My thing was that I pushed, I challenged guys. I wanted to know how far they could be pushed. My mind-set was that this would make them better players on Sunday.

My first season with Dallas in 1992, our defensive line coach was Butch Davis. Now, I like Butch, and he was a heck of a coach. He ended up becoming a head coach in both the NFL and college and deservedly so. I respected him as much as any position coach in my career. Still, he was like anyone else. If he pushed me, it wasn't going to end well.

After practices I would stay on the field and work with the younger linemen. And this often meant showing up late to Butch's position meetings. And he was always bitching about me being late. But it wasn't like I was sleeping or clowning around. I was working with my teammates, trying to make them better. Well, I was quickly becoming tired of his yelling. So one day I'm taking a shower after practice, and Butch is going on and on about I'm going to be late for the meeting. Hell with that. I kept showering, and he left and started the meeting. I finished my shower, wrapped a towel around my head, walked into the meeting room, and laid down on the floor—*buck ass naked*. He turned around after drawing some play on the board and certainly appeared shocked. He stormed out of the room.

This got Butch and Jimmy Johnson pissed at me. And I decided to shut down. I didn't talk to anyone for two weeks. Like no one, not my teammates, not my coaches. I came to practice, I played hard during the games, but I wasn't communicating with anyone. Screw them. We were playing Denver in early December, and I'm taking a piss before the game. Jimmy walks over to me as I'm finishing and says, "You keep this silent treatment shit up, and your career is going to end up with that piss of yours—down the drain." And he flushes the urinal and walks away. He was right, too. I wasn't hurting them by not talking, I was hurting my teammates, my defensive line guys who depended on me to break down film and work with them. I was being a world-class ass.

So yeah, I did a lot of stuff. I'm not playing myself off as the angel in this, but at least I have the balls to look somebody in the eye if I'm going to say something. That's the only thing I don't like about some of these stories. You have some unnamed source and you get Tom, Dick, and Harry to talk about it. Maybe Charles was a butthole to them, and this is the way they've decided to get back at him. Because once you put it in a book, it's there forever.

I don't care. At the end of the day, I don't care because the people who know me, and I hope the majority of those who played with me do, they know my character.

Then again, maybe I do care, and it's just easier to say I don't.

Hell, I didn't know who I was back then. Even today there are times when I don't know. Who the hell am I? Am I Charles, Chuck, or Charlie? I tell people there are three of me. Charles is the one that's stable, somewhat normal. Charlie is the sensitive one that cries a lot, and Chuck is the asshole. So when I say or do something crazy, when I regroup, I tell people, "That's Chuck, and he went that way, down the street. It's good now." I don't like Chuck. He's a bad dude. Charlie is okay, but Charles is the man I try to be. It just happened a lot less back during my playing career.

★ ★ ★

Early on with the 49ers, I remember going to a bachelor party. They had a bunch of strippers and they tied them up, ripped their clothes off, and then poured tequila all over them. Then they took turns licking it all off. I was like, *wow, damn.* I hadn't been exposed to much at that point, and now all of this stuff was suddenly happening. I remember who was there, and guess what, it's no one's damn business. For the record there is nothing like a bachelor party with NFL players in the 1980s. All of the drugs, alcohol, and naked women, no one would believe half of it.

I remember we went to Las Vegas—this was also during my first year or two with San Francisco—and some guys went out and bought cocaine and got busted. It was taken care of, and we were able to fly home without it going public. That night was a mess. Everything was easy. You didn't have to ask for anything; it was always there and it was constant.

There were guys doing steroids everywhere you looked. When the steroid guys would have to take tests, they would take a fake penis, put somebody's urine in it, and then squeeze that urine into the piss cup. This was before they would go and watch the guy taking his piss. I guess they just trusted dudes back then. Not a good idea.

I must have led the league in giving my urine to teammates because everyone was sure I wasn't taking anything. I was the smallest defensive lineman in the league. Hell, Carolina Panthers quarterback Cam Newton is like 30 pounds heavier than I was for the majority of my career. You walk through an NFL locker room, and it doesn't take more than a few seconds to see who is taking performance enhancement drugs and who isn't.

A lot of my former teammates who told stories, they obviously didn't like me. Hey, I could say a lot of things about them that are 100 percent accurate, but I choose not to because we had a code: what happens in the locker room stays in the locker room. I understand I was a hard man. I was an extremely hard, angry man. I attacked everything from their kids to their momma to them. There were no boundaries for me, and looking back, I understand why they did it.

But I was a sick man. I was dealing with an illness. And it made me do some crazy stuff. I was always pushing, I was always being aggressive, I was always trying to find the boundaries.

It didn't help that I was a clown by nature. I've been a clown my entire life, long before I was Charles Haley, the football player. I was the kid in first grade doing whatever I could to make people laugh. I love hearing people laugh; maybe it's a positive reinforcement kind of thing. It makes me feel good when I make someone laugh.

And I'm no stand-up comic, so I talk about people. I hone in on their weakness and make fun of it. A dude talks funny. Bam, I'm there with an impersonation. A dude has a big nose. Cue up the best Rudolph jokes I can think of. I didn't have a filter either. That was the problem. Busting someone's balls can be funny. Most of it is totally within the boundaries of a locker room, a group of buddies. But other stuff is best not spoken. I didn't understand that.

There are some stories about me that are just fantasy. I never ejaculated around any of my teammates—or on them for that matter. *What the hell?* You're going to tell me that a man is going to let another man ejaculate on him with no problem? I don't give a damn if I weigh 100 pounds. If some man comes up to me ready to burst, guess what? Before that happens I'm taking him down. I'd rather get my ass whooped than any situation like that.

Other incidents were misunderstandings—at least to me they were. Here's the thing, when you are bipolar and not taking medication, it's kind of like selective memory. I did a lot of stuff and a lot of stuff I'm certainly not proud of. When my kids, or someday my grandchildren,

Google my name, those stories are going to be there. I hear people tell their stories about me. But this is the God's honest truth, the best way I can explain it: I remember every slight against me, what people did to me, but I don't remember a lot of what I did to others. I get different versions of different actions from my playing days, but more times than not, it doesn't match what I remember.

I think my biggest frustration is that I cared for a lot of my former teammates, then and now, and because of my issues, that probably was lost on them. You can take whatever you want from relationships, from being a part of a team. A lot of teammates thought I was crazy because I pushed them hard to win instead of realizing that I cared about them. I guess I didn't always show that, outside of a few guys—close friends like Ronnie Lott, Keena Turner, Leon Lett, and Tony Tolbert—so the rest of them probably have all different kinds of ideas and memories about me. But again, it is what it is.

When I see former teammates, I always apologize even if I don't remember doing anything to them. I just figured I must have. Most of them are pretty cool. I guess winning helps that when you look back. If we finished 6–10 every year and never won a Super Bowl, I'm sure teammates, coaches, everyone would maybe not be as forgiving. There was a means to my end.

Being a smart player helped me, too. Outside of my BS and clowning around, I talked a lot of football with my teammates, my coaches. It wasn't like I was crazy every day. I had control of me for the most part, particularly on the field. I remember Coach Walsh told me one time, he said, "Charles, we cut dumb players. Not because we don't like them, but dumb players cost you games with dumb mistakes. And if they are on the field with the opportunity to make a dumb play, that's on us as coaches. Even if a guy has potential, we cut them."

I wasn't going to be one of those guys, which is why I watched so much film. And by studying what every one of my teammates did, I could have a conversation with any of them about football. I could ask them questions about why they did this or that. I wasn't just running around the film rooms naked all day. I would pick and choose when to step out of my comfort zone. Well, I guess the bipolar chose. I'm just saying that there were a lot of good, productive days for me as a teammate. But those stories aren't told all that much.

I honestly viewed the world as being against me. My mind-set was that everyone woke up in the morning, collectively looked around nodding their heads, and thought, *how can we screw Charles today?* That was where the rage came from. It felt like me against the world.

And after I left the 49ers, and they did a kind of character assassination on me, that only escalated. They tried to say everything about me was negative, or maybe that's how it was communicated. They made everyone in the league fear me with these crazy-ass stories, a lot more than what actually happened.

At the time I don't think the 49ers wanted to see me succeed. They wanted me to fail, especially playing for a conference rival in the Cowboys. If I continued to be successful on the field for Dallas, that was going to reflect poorly on San Francisco's decision to deal me for a few draft picks, so they tarnished my reputation. I guess that's business, as they say.

I'm not mad about it any longer. I know those who made the decisions with the 49ers. They knew I could do a lot of things on the field to help the team, but they couldn't find a way to control me, and that's the bottom line. I find myself saying this a lot, but it's true: it was all about control. They couldn't control me, and sometimes I couldn't control me.

I don't know if my teammates, be it high school, college, or in the NFL, were intimidated by me. All I knew was that if any of them put their hands on me, we're going to settle this up regardless. That's how I was raised. You can lock the doors or whatever, I'm going to get your ass. As I mentioned, I wasn't one of the guys in the locker room. So that intimidation, or whatever you want to call it, helped me from a standpoint of them not being able to get close to me. That's important, too. I didn't want people to know what was going on in my mind. There was a lot of stuff going on in my head, and outside of Karen, my mother, maybe Ronnie, I wasn't going to confide in or trust anyone else. My teammates were there for football, not to be my psychologist.

For the majority of my NFL career, really from my second season in 1987, it was "Charles is out of control. Charles is not dealing with his issues. Charles is definitely not in charge of his emotions." I wish I could take some of that back.

Instead, I think I came to like the reputation and almost ran with it. I'm not saying it was all an act, just that, hey, it couldn't hurt for them to all think I was crazy. And that affected my ability to have friendships like the other guys did. I probably walked out of the league with only a handful of guys, definitely less than a dozen, who were friends. I rubbed a lot of folks wrong with my actions and words. That's what I regret. I can be a nice guy. I think if they knew me today, that would be a lot different.

I also regret verbally attacking coaches. That was beyond wrong. Those guys were the coaches, the ones trying to help us win, and I was always making their lives a nightmare. Even Coach Walsh probably had some frustration with me, though I was always on my best behavior with him.

The coaches put up with a lot. I can't change it. The only thing I can do now is say how much regret I have. When I see these guys, my ex-teammates and former coaches, I tell them how much regret I have. I'm not sorry; I regret the actions. There's a difference. It's so easy to say I'm sorry, but what does that mean? What significance does it carry? When you say you regret something, then you have to talk specifically about what you did and how badly you feel about it. But your regrets in life are never forgotten—by you or those who were affected by your actions. I don't like the word *sorry*.

Not being friendly with a lot of my teammates is definitely on me, and it's twofold. There were the issues and the reputation, but I also never looked for friends. When it did happen, it just kind of happened. Take Leon, who is one of the most talented defensive linemen I've ever seen play. He was so quick that we called him the "Big Cat." He was in his second season with the Cowboys when I arrived in 1992, and at first we had a working relationship. They had him drive me to the hotel that first day I flew in. I was teaching him stuff from that first time we met. Leon is really quiet, more so back then than now, but in time our relationship transformed into love, where he knows I love him with all my heart and that I will always be there for him.

When Leon was suspended for failing a drug test, I guess it was 1995, once I heard the news I immediately left our practice facility in Valley Ranch and drove to his house. I spent the day with him and tracked down Jimmy Johnson also. Jimmy was with the Miami Dolphins at the time, but he called me back and spoke with Leon for 15 minutes.

I was always bringing my kids to Leon's house so we could swim. He wouldn't even be home half the time. Leon overcame his issues, returned to school, and graduated and is now an assistant coach with the Dallas Cowboys. The first phone call he gets every Monday morning after games is me with my notes from watching the game. Leon is one of my closest friends.

I obviously had some trust issues when I was playing, probably still do, but on a much, much lesser scale. The number of teammates I trusted back in the day—I mean trusted without a doubt—is a list that can be counted on one hand. There was Ronnie, there was Leon, and then there was Tony Tolbert, a heck of a defensive end who spent nine seasons with the Cowboys from 1989 to 1997. Both he and Leon became Pro Bowl selections after I showed up, which I took a lot of pride in. They both were always asking me questions and watching film with me.

Off the field, Tony and I came from the same cloth. We came from smaller towns, were both undersized, not heavily recruited. I am pretty sure that the team was hoping Tony would keep me calm and under control, as he's a mellow dude, but he never tried to guide me in that direction. He didn't try to change me. Everyone was trying to tame me, telling me how to act. Tony just treated me like a peer.

We would sit for hours and talk about our backgrounds, how people always picked on us when we were growing up, how no one thought we would ever make it because we were small, all that stuff. It was like he had lived the same life as I did before we met. We went to smaller colleges, too. He went to UTEP, where my son ended up going.

Even though no one believed in us, that didn't intimidate Tony or me. It actually just provided motivation. Every single time that we heard we wouldn't do anything, that we wouldn't amount to anything, that just made us work harder. Tony and I each experienced so much of that, so there was a natural bond. At the end of the day, God was right. He told Tony and me to stay the course, say our prayers, which I know I did every night, and prove all of our naysayers wrong.

Know what's somewhat interesting about my playing days? For all the stories and such, I never got in trouble with the NFL, like never. No fines. No suspensions. I wasn't a troublemaker in that sense. And while I had some serious issues with alcohol and drugs after my playing career, that wasn't something I was really into at the time. I drank a little bit, and had a few incidents with that, and I smoked marijuana every once in a while but certainly not regularly.

For me, once the NFL came in with having probable cause to drug test someone, I backed off big time. When they introduced the drug tests after I was in the league for a few years, my mood swings were left and right, so every day I was a case for probable cause. Because of that, I made sure I stayed clean. They came to me one morning when I was in San Francisco and said they were going to test me, and I said, "Damn, well, I can tell you I'm dirty right now. I smoked some weed last week." I remember those words coming out of my mouth and just having a realization, like *wow, what am I doing?* Fortunately, you don't get suspended for your first offense, but the decisions, my actions, they have real consequences because I already had a few kids and Karen, and this dumb-ass stuff I was doing could affect them. That's when it was like, yo, Charles, time to grow up.

This was kind of like at James Madison, that first week of school, when I realized that I wasn't prepared academically, so I decided to make some changes and work my ass off. That was the deal then. I didn't want my kids to have this image of their father as a guy who did drugs or was in trouble. Now, that eventually blew up where my kids did end up seeing a side of me that wasn't nice.

There was another factor, too. Yeah, I didn't want to be embarrassed, have anyone look down on me, but there was also the money. I have a family, and you know what? I don't have time for the NFL to take any of my money. I don't have time for any team to take any of my money. My thing was: first one to work, last one to leave, so how the hell are you going to fine me?

Yes, I could be a world-class ass, but I also taught my teammates every damn thing I knew about rushing the passer, about the game itself. I was all for seeing the guy behind me on the depth chart improve because it makes us a better football team, and it forces me to become a better player. It pushes me. If I'm at the top of the food chain and no one is chewing on my ass, then I'm not going to improve.

A lot of people never understood that. Some veterans wanted to keep their secrets, keep the younger guys down, and maybe keep their jobs for another year. To me, that was crap. I wanted to win. And to win every guy on the team needs to be maximizing his talent, his abilities. I wanted to teach them everything. I would sit in meeting rooms and watch film with them, go over the weaknesses of the guy they were going up against. I would sit in the film room with the quarterbacks and offensive linemen to give them another perspective.

Most of the guys didn't like me, and I knew that. My own teammates, even the defensive linemen, a lot of them didn't like me personally, and I understand that. But I hope looking back that they understand what my motivation was. I hope that they understand my bottom line was winning. And we won a lot of ballgames.

Chapter 2

Growing Up in Gladys

WHEN YOU GROW UP POOR and just about everyone else around you is poor, it doesn't really register that you're poor. I mean, we just didn't know how other people were living. We didn't know our world wasn't normal, middle-class America, which, looking back, is probably a good thing. It probably made it easier on us.

Make no mistake, though, my family was poor growing up in Gladys, Virginia, a small town of less than 4,000 folks located in the central part of the state, not far from Lynchburg. Hell, I was never more than 30 miles from my house until I left for college. There were no vacations or going to see a ballgame. We were trying to survive. I was the fourth of five boys—James, George Jr., Lawrence, Charles, and David—born to George and Virginia Haley. My parents worked their asses off. They had the kind of manual labor jobs that cause your body to ache. I know because I worked with them sometimes, and even as a young kid, I was hurting for certain, let me tell you.

My dad is like a picture on the wall. He'll walk in a room and stand right by the wall, and after about two or three minutes, you won't even know he's there. He's an introvert, beyond shy, but he led by example. My brothers and I would go to work with him, and he would work like you can't envision a man working. He worked as a machine operator for a fiberglass company. That was his full-time job, and he cut down pulpwood on the side. He'd bring us along to lift the pulpwood, which is what remains after you cut down pine trees. It's kind of like logging. Let me promise you something, it was tough work.

My father is a big man, 6'2", 250 pounds, and we would see him pick up these huge-trunked trees, big ol' logs. He'd put them on his shoulder, walk them down, and throw them on a truck. And being the no-nonsense guy he is, it was like a routine. When he finished walking them down, you could see his footprints in the ground. They were that heavy.

Then you tried it, and, damn, it was totally exhausting. Later on, when I was running sprints or drills or whatever on the football field, I'd remember how my father somehow eliminated the pain he must have been feeling. I guess that was an inspiration. While working for him, I was just miserable, but it served multiple purposes. First, I saw just how hard my father worked, and second, I learned I certainly didn't want to be doing that with my life.

My father taught us what hard work was. The kind of hard work where the alternative is not having food on the table. I've never heard him complain either. Growing up, my dad was really good at basketball, but his parents died young, and his older brother was taking care of him. When he turned 16, the decision was pretty clear. He dropped out of school and went to work.

Maybe it was like this in a lot of families, but my father wouldn't spank us. Our mom took care of that. My father tried one time and ended up crying. He literally—I remember this so clearly—was crying while he spanked us, and I'm thinking, *wow, I like this*. By the time he got to me, the fourth kid, I got only one, and he was done. He never touched us again.

My mother, Virginia, can be mean. I tell people she's too mean to die. Even today at 70-something years old, she's no joke. She's not putting up with anything. But I love her so much. We talk almost every day; we always have, even during college and during my career. She didn't go past the sixth grade and she wanted more for her kids than she had. I love her to death because she's done one hell of a good job.

Let me promise you this, though, my mom is one tough woman. I guess she had to be to raise five boys. She doesn't give empty promises either. She also has some size—5'10", maybe 180 pounds. My dad was always working two, three jobs at a time, and so my mom was the heavy hand, the disciplinarian. But she was always there for us, too. She always made us look after each other. Her motto was if somebody hit one of your brothers and you're standing there and don't retaliate, you better not come home because she was going to lay the wood.

Just like from my father, I learned and inherited toughness from her. She played softball when I was growing up, and there's this one story I have never forgotten. She cut some ligaments in her hand so she couldn't make a fist, but she would still go out there and play. She was tough. She would play first base. I think watching her go through some of that, seeing how fierce she was, helped me later in my career. As a child she was badly burned during a woodstove accident and has scars to this day on her arms and legs, but she never said a word about them. There is nothing in this world my mother is afraid of.

Besides raising my four brothers and me, my mother also worked full time as a sprayer on the assembly line at a furniture manufacturer. She dropped out of school early, too, so she could start working, but she went back and earned her GED. That was important to her. She was always preaching education to us. She wanted her boys to have opportunities in this world that she didn't.

I've never heard either one of my parents talk about what they've been through. I asked my mom one time, and she said, "Why?" I told her I just wanted to know, and she said, "Well, let me tell you, I'm not going to give you a reason to hate anybody because of the past." So she never told us anything. My dad has talked some the last two or three years. He's talked a little bit about some things he went through, how he grew up, losing his parents, what he had to do, the sacrifices at a young age. Most of us are just getting started at 16, and he was working two jobs.

My mother made me and my brothers play sports. That's how it was growing up in my neighborhood. Everyone went outside after break- fast and we were either working or playing sports. With my brothers out, I couldn't stay home, which oftentimes I would have preferred.

Once we were old enough, which was like at age six or seven, when we weren't at school or church or eating or sleeping, we were outside. Everything one of the five Haley brothers did, the rest had to do. That's how my mother wanted it.

I was fat growing up. When we started playing organized football, I was always that kid who had to put on two plastic jackets and run around to lose weight in order to play with my age group. Football was definitely a part of my childhood. The only problem was that I was no good. I wasn't good at anything, and my brothers were good at everything. So I pretty much became a class clown. I always called myself Charlie Brown. You know when he goes to kick the ball, and Lucy picks the ball up? That was me, though more times than not, I was just falling down on my own from being so awkward and clumsy.

I had big feet. My feet just kept growing, so that didn't help. I was wearing a size-10 in elementary school. I had to come home, take my good shoes off, and put the old ones on. I went barefoot a lot. I used to stub my toe all the time. I was a mess.

When we picked teams at school or in the neighborhood, I was never picked, even by my own brothers. I remember all that stuff. You never forget those childhood scars. Maybe we aren't equipped to deal with them at that age, but I just never felt a part of any group—even with my brothers. No one wanted me on their teams, and everyone made fun of me 24 hours a day, seven days a week.

I mean, there's nothing worse than not feeling like a part of your own family, especially as a kid. And because of that, there was a lot of hate inside of me. It kept building and building. As far back as I can remember, too, I just always felt like everyone was against me. This lasted throughout my NFL career, and I'm trying to fight those demons to this very day. I'm trying every day to take little steps and talk about my childhood during counseling. We talk for hours about me letting it go. It's from another time, another place. Still, there is a lot of pain there for me.

I was bullied a lot. When I had enough self-esteem to stand up for myself and fight back, then that became another problem entirely because I became the bully, and then my trust factor for people went way down. And honestly, it wasn't high to begin with. I'm one of those guys who is going to watch. I'm going to watch you, and as the words come out of your mouth, I'm going to see if it turns to action. I don't like leaving stuff to chance. Yeah, yeah, I know, just because I was bullied as a kid didn't give me the excuse to bully others as I became older and even throughout my playing career. There's a lot of guilt there with me.

We played pickup football on Sundays after church and during the summers, too. My brothers and I were always on the same team. We'd play wherever—dirt fields, hay fields, cornfields, parking lots—there wasn't a whole lot of grass where I'm from. We'd spend a few minutes clearing the glass and rocks as best we could and then start playing. We always played tackle, too. None of this two-hand tag stuff. It was fun. Those are some of my happier memories of growing up.

My favorite games would be against other neighborhoods. Basically, it was all of my brothers and then my uncles, and then we had a couple of more guys. It was a great time. And we had a gameplan. We would let them score at first, give them a little confidence, but the next time they had the ball, we would dive at their feet. Then when they went to jump over us, we would clothesline their ass. Sometimes, if we didn't like them, we would hold them up by the legs so we could take shots at their necks. We would send them to the hospital on occasion and we'd always win in the end, whether by forfeit because of injuries or on the scoreboard.

* * *

My grandparents all died young. I vaguely remember my grandmother. I think she passed when I was five or six. There were uncles, aunts, and cousins all around us, same street, same block. The Haleys and the

Browns, my mother's maiden name, all lived within a quarter mile of each other. I remember as young kids we would go half a mile down to a spring and get water for our older relatives, including my grandmother before she died.

We didn't have indoor plumbing at that point, so a road trip for me was going to a neighbor's well to fill up the bucket for the outhouse. We would bathe in a tub filled up with water from the well. It was obviously a different time and place. This would have been around 1970, give or take a few years. One of our neighbors did have running water, so I knew it existed, but they didn't have five kids one year apart each. They had more financial flexibility. Our flexibility was whether we were using milk or water on our cereal.

The road we lived on was paved, though, and we got bikes one year for Christmas. We would ride them up and down the street all day until it was too dark to see. Of course, one of us would get mad at another, and we'd bust a tire or mess up a rim. You know how brothers are, right? My mother would also buy these board games, and I'd lose and throw away all the pieces because I was mad. I never did like losing.

Our lives became simpler when I was around nine years old. Through all the hard work of my parents, we were able to move half a mile down the street into a house with running water, so everything changed. That was huge. It was a two-bedroom house, so we had bunk beds. As I mentioned, my brothers were hard on me. They used to beat me up. I think I might have set the beds on fire. Who am I kidding? I know I set the beds on fire. My brothers pounded on me for years. I was never close to any of them. I'm still not.

I had some other issues with fire. I guess I was kind of a junior pyromaniac. When I was a kid, I set the woods on fire down at my grandmother's place, and my grandmother slapped me. I thought she might have slapped my head off. It was one dumb thing after another with me.

Along with the new house, we had our first television. That was like a whole new world, not that I was able to watch it much. My mother mostly watched it. She'd watch *Days of our Lives* and all of that crap. I just wanted to watch cartoons, but with all the chores, school, homework, and playing sports, there wasn't much time for the tube. Maybe it's because I didn't really have that typical childhood, but I still enjoy watching cartoons. I watched them all the time during my playing days. For hours. I'd wake up and watch Bugs Bunny. Anyhow, on one television we had while growing up, we needed to go outside and turn the antenna to find channels and get a decent reception, no matter what the weather was. If my mother wanted to watch her show, she was going to find the channel. That was the worst part of the whole deal right there. My favorite memories are when my mother would be cooking, and we'd be at the table doing our homework, and the TV would be on. We were kind of all watching it as a family, even if it was mostly background noise. But we didn't do that much because my father was usually working. There was always just the one TV.

We never watched sports. The first full NFL game I ever saw, on television or in person, was one I played in. I do remember seeing "Mean" Joe Greene on the TV. He's the reason I started playing linebacker. When that kid gave him that Coke and he threw the jersey, to me, that was another world. My parents went bowling, and the TV was on, and there he was. I didn't know who a lot of people were outside of my neighborhood and school. I wasn't aware of athletes, actors, and musicians. That was for other people. We didn't have access to that. We didn't see movies. But my brothers were all impressed by "Mean" Joe, so I was too. When I came into the league, I remember teammates and the media talking about all of these famous players, and I had no idea who they were. I only knew Joe Greene. For me, he was the NFL.

When I was younger, my mom, who was a Southern Baptist, beat Jesus Christ into my brothers and me because if we made noise, laughed, joked, or fell asleep in church or Sunday school when we weren't supposed to, she would slap us upside the head and say, "Wait until you get home." She wanted us to pay attention, and there were consequences to not doing so.

I read all the time, mostly the Bible, but I read some other books. I think more or less the church and Sunday school taught me how to read because schools kept kicking me out. I was always mesmerized by the books in the Bible, about all the heroes, so I always picked myself to be one of the heroes in the Bible, even as I grew older. We were a religious family. Honestly, that wasn't a choice. In my mother's house, under her roof, you were going to church. I didn't mind it, though. My brothers and I sang in the choir, and the people there were nice. When I was younger, I wanted to be a preacher. Yes, Charles Haley the preacher. I would even try to talk like the Southern Baptist preachers.

I remember we were baptized in a creek. So we go down—I can't swim—and they tell me to hold my breath. They wait until after it rains so the water is high. They dump you backward, and you see logs, you see limbs and everything else going by. That is faith right there. They have the ceremonies in the church now, but back then we had to go to the creek to get baptized. That was a moving moment for me.

Middle school ended up being a turning point for me in my life for multiple reasons. First, I was growing so fast that some of that baby fat started to fall off me. I think because of the work with my father, carrying the trees, all the exercise running around and riding our bikes, I was becoming stronger, too.

That's when the terrorizing started to shift. They weren't coming after me any longer. I wouldn't give them the chance. Also, I asked God one Sunday in church, I said, "I'm tired of being different. I know I'm not the smartest guy in the world, but just give me one thing I can be great at." I promised him I would work my tail off in whatever that one thing was. Just give me the opportunity. And he gave me football. The very next time we played, I was still the last one picked, but that never happened again. I was scoring touchdowns and hitting everything and everybody that moved.

Finding something I was good at didn't mean I was staying out of trouble, though. I was always trying to make people laugh in class, which didn't help me with my teachers. And then I was getting into fights before and after school—and sometimes during. I was suspended all the time. My mom was at every parent-teacher conference. She was there, and there were consequences. By my recollection those consequences were damn painful.

When the teacher said I didn't listen, that I acted up, and disrupted the class, my mom would just slap me right then and there, and the teacher never blinked. The teacher would just keep telling my mother what I did wrong, and the slaps would just keep coming. It was like, *okay, yeah, give it to him*. It was like the teacher was enjoying watching me get mine. Maybe they figured that was for all of the trouble I gave them. Still, I have a special and deep bond with my mom. Then and now.

I used to get in so much trouble at that age. My father once lost a good part-time job because the son of his boss hit me with a water hose, and he went up there and scared the bejesus out of him. And after a few schools expelled me for fighting, I would already be in trouble at new schools because they just figured I was going to start a fight or retaliate anyway. I probably was going to, but they didn't even give me the opportunity.

When I was growing up, I was always mad—like every day. One day, I picked up a .22 pistol in a neighbor's yard. Well, maybe I didn't just stumble upon it. I took it, I stole it, and I brought it home. I had never shot a gun. I was around 13 years old. And I remember looking down the barrel and I pulled the trigger by accident. It blew my eardrum, and then I realized there was a bullet in the wall.

Looking back, I hadn't planned on stealing it. I hadn't visualized taking it beforehand. Hell, though, if I took it, then I must have had some intention. No one steals a gun and finds himself looking down the barrel for no reason. God took all that away from me, though, because a .22 doesn't jump. But the bullet missed me. It completely blew my right eardrum, but I knew God had me.

I told my mother when she came home and gave her the gun to return.

Just like when I set those woods on fire or my brothers' bunk beds, I don't know why I did it. There was so much hate and anger going through my heart and mind. Most times, when I was being destructive or self-destructive, I would be almost outside of myself. Ten minutes later I would be like, "Wait, what just happened? There's no way I did that."

I'm just glad that I have the kind of relationship with my mom that I could always depend on her like that. She's my lifeline. She knows every dirty, dumb secret that I have. I will call and tell her after. I have put a lot of stress on that woman. Let's be real honest about this: without my momma, I'd be in jail or dead.

At that point at 13, 14 years old, I'd had enough of everybody picking on me for how I talked, for being overweight when I was younger, for not being that smart, for being clumsy, or maybe it was just some good-natured ribbing that I should have been able to deal with. In my mind, though, I was going to start giving those who came after me some consequences.

My freshman year at William Campbell High School in Gladys, I was 14 years old and wore a size-14 shoe. My feet never stopped growing until I was in the NFL, finally maxing out at a size-17. I didn't play all that much on the middle school team, mostly because I was always goofing around and not respecting my coach. My mother even yelled at him during halftime of a game once. And this is embarrassing to admit, but I honestly didn't like being hit by the bigger kids, so I wasn't in a rush to be on the field. That made me angry. Not at anyone else, but at myself. I wanted my mother to come to my games and be proud of me, so I started working harder. I was running every minute I could. I kept my mouth shut at practice…well, at least for me.

After starting both ways on the junior varsity team my freshman year of high school, I started on the varsity team as a sophomore, playing linebacker, tight end, and kicker. Yes, kicker, which was problematic with my ever-expanding feet. They would go to nearby colleges to get cleats for me. They were these hideous orange and yellow cleats. Those must have been the ugliest cleats the game of football has ever seen.

And I won the district's Defensive Player of the Year, while my brother Lawrence won Offensive Player of the Year. I played basketball in the winter and threw the discus in the spring. There was always something going on, but football was my love. This didn't make my life with school any easier. There were weeks when I was suspended for three days, but it always seemed to work out so that I came back just in time to be eligible for football games. I knew what I was to them. They were trying to control me, and no one was controlling me at that point in my life.

I think that's where my distaste for coaches started because of the actions that they took in trying to get me under their control. I doubt there are records on this, but I'm thinking I spent more time suspended than actually in school those four years. I worked hard enough when I was there. I was always interested in learning stuff and I knew my reading and writing wasn't where it should have been. Maybe I did enough to pass, maybe the teachers just passed me to get me the hell out of their class, or maybe they wanted to keep me playing football. I don't know; I never asked.

The head football coach was named Ronald Cox, and we didn't get along most of the time. One of his problems was that my brothers and I couldn't work out with the team during the summer. Hell, he must have known that I would have much rather been playing ball. We were working in the tobacco fields, so we could buy clothes and whatnot.

There was one summer when we, all five of the Haley brothers, worked on a farm. We did every job known to man. We used to herd the cows and we had to cut the fence down. It was an electric fence. We had to disconnect it until the cows would go back in, shoo them back in, fix the fence, and then jog home probably five, six miles. We worked in the silos. I tell my mom all the time that I came out of her womb working.

We never did the weightlifting and running before school because we were carrying trees with my father. But we were working our asses off and we were in as good of shape as anyone.

Still, that seemed to bother everyone, so the coaches took it out on us. They said they wouldn't give us any awards and all that stuff. In the end who else was going to win? So we still won them.

College never entered my mind during my sophomore and junior years. Coaches, guidance counselors, teachers—someone should have talked with us. No one from our family or neighborhood had ever gone to college, but with how my brothers and I were playing football, there was an opportunity. We were the best players. We were All-State, All-American. Whatever it was, we were there. Then a few college coaches came around at the end of my junior year. We had our backs up against the wall. The alternative is working in a factory like my parents or going into farming. I could have been milking cows for the last 35 years, picking up pig shit.

By this time I was about 150 pounds, maybe 155. I was just running around at middle linebacker, side-to-side, dropping into coverage, blitzing, though teams didn't throw much. I was learning to read plays, looking at the quarterback's eyes. At tight end I was mostly blocking. As a senior I put on a little more weight and was probably playing at 170 pounds on most Friday nights.

As you can imagine, there wasn't a whole bunch of college coaches looking for 6'4", 170-pound middle linebackers, even in the early

1980s. And I was also playing for a small school. This is decades before scouting services on the Internet and all that stuff. There was a real chance no one would discover me. I often think there had to be kids out there who possessed the same talent as me who never got their shot. It only takes one, though. And Danny Wilmer was my one. We aren't writing this book without Coach Wilmer. Heck, I might still be struggling to read a book without that man.

He has an eye for talent, having signed a bunch of multiple NFL Pro Bowl selections like Tiki and Ronde Barber, Gary Clark, and Heath Miller. The story goes that another high school coach, from Danville, Virginia, told him to watch some film on me. Coach Wilmer had no clue who I was; no one did. But Wilmer decided to check me out, and I guess on this one play, I ran down some state champion sprinter from behind. You probably don't see linebackers chase down wide receivers every day. At the time Wilmer was an assistant coach at James Madison University, which is about two hours north of Gladys in Harrisonburg, Virginia.

Coach Wilmer—he has the biggest head I have ever seen in my life—came down to William Campbell. He had this chew in his mouth and he said, "Son, we want you to come to JMU to play." And they offered me and my brother Lawrence scholarships. My brother didn't accept. He didn't think he was ready for college. He ended up never going.

So Coach Wilmer comes to my house, and people never sit in the living room in black folks' houses unless it's a special occasion. Coach told my momma that he's going to take care of me, that I'm going to get a great education, and he promised her that I was going to graduate. My mom ate it all up because of her goals for us. There was nothing she wanted more than to see one of her boys go off to college.

I think my father was proud, too. We're old school, where fathers and sons don't talk about that stuff. He didn't teach us. It's not like that where we lived. But he put up this plywood backboard with a basket. The court itself was dirt. On weekends, when he wasn't working, he would come out and play with us. You would watch and learn.

Honestly, I was just happy to get any time with my dad. He was never able to come see me play, not in high school or college. And I wanted to show him what I could do. He read the paper, so he knew that the Haley boys were the whole team. They didn't call us by name; they would just call us the Haley boys. Maybe Charles was too difficult for the sportswriters to spell.

A lot of people think bad of my father for not coming to games, but you know what? He told me he loved me. That took a lot for him, for any father back in those days to say something like that. But my father, he said, "Son, I love you. I'd love to go see you play, but I have to work," and I respected him for it. The man has been an inspiration for me since Day One.

So the only two schools recruiting me through my senior season were James Madison and Liberty University. Then came the East vs. West All-Star Game, and when I get there, all the guys from the big high schools are playing linebacker. So they made me play tight end, and I caught everything. I've got great hands. I caught everything that they threw, and then all of a sudden, every college there wanted me. The bigger ones wanted me to come play tight end, but I don't like getting hit. That crap hurts.

The attention was nice for a few weeks, but there was never any doubt. They could have offered me a scholarship to the University of the Playboy Mansion, and I was going to James Madison because of Coach Wilmer.

The funny thing is, when I first arrived on campus, some of the coaches started talking about me playing tight end, and I said, "No problem guys, I'm going home. Enjoy the season." They let me stay at linebacker.

I was the first kid in my neighborhood to go to college. That was neat for my parents. For all of us, really. College, at the time, from where I was from, was like going to the moon. It was that unrealistic. Most folks in Gladys never want to leave, and that's fine. That's their prerogative. For me, I wanted out in the worst way. I couldn't go back. I needed to escape, I needed to find a better life. And also, there were a lot of painful memories for me back there.

Even to this day, I don't go home much. I try to get back two or three times a year. I still have a hard time with my brothers because of the things they've done to me. I haven't come to grips with that yet. I can deal with them, I love them, but I just can't find a reason, outside of seeing my mother, that makes me want to visit Gladys. I really don't have any friends there.

I've just never bonded with my brothers. We don't even talk on the phone much. I'm hoping through therapy and counseling that I'm able to overcome that and move on, maybe have those relationships you hear about other brothers having. I have to stop being angry at stuff that took place 40 years ago. When I went into the NFL, I helped my brothers any way I could financially. And all of our kids went to college, so my mother and father broke the cycle. They created better lives and opportunities for those who came after them. That's the American dream, right?

Strangely, my most profound memory of Gladys has nothing to do with football. When I was 16 years old, standing in my front yard, my mother came around the corner in her car, hit the ditch right across the street from us, and really hurt herself. At that moment I had a vision that I would one day tear that bank down and I would own everything across the street. And now I do.

I was able to build a new house for my parents. I offered to build one for them anywhere they wanted. They settled on the same street in Gladys where I grew up. And it took my father years to move in. He spent most of his time at the two-bedroom house across the street. Some people are just comfortable in what they know.

Chapter 3

Opportunity of a Lifetime

IT'S SAFE TO SAY that the people of James Madison University certainly didn't know what to expect with my arrival in the fall of 1982. Even more so, though, I had absolutely zero idea of what to expect. Outside of the football stuff, which was fine, I was probably more prepared to live among the Amish than what was awaiting me.

My challenges had nothing to do with James Madison, which is a beautiful place with green grass (not the kind you smoke, though they had that, too) and buildings that we certainly didn't have in Gladys. Remember, we never traveled anywhere, so this was a new world for me. Anywhere was going to be a new world for me.

I didn't have any white friends when I was growing up. Our town was segregated. But when I went to college, 90 to 95 percent of the campus was white. Yet they didn't treat me or make me feel like people did when I was growing up. Everyone treated me with respect. No one looked down on me. So that was a big part of my new world, just feeling like another person, a peer even.

Also, there was just being away from home. The farthest I had ever been was Lynchburg, which is about 35 minutes outside of my hometown. And then I had to go all the way up to James Madison in Harrisonburg, which was like a two-and-a-half-hour drive. I remember when my mother dropped me off for my freshman year. She read me the riot act the entire ride there. I mean, she chewed my ass out in ways you couldn't imagine. She told me that my room was gone back home, and that I could come back to visit, but that I wasn't staying. I knew she wasn't kidding around. It was her way of letting me know that this was my chance in life, this was my time to change my world, our world, and there was no running home. There was no failing.

So there we are, standing in my room on campus. My mother fixes the bed all nice. I'm scared as crap, and she sends me out to get my footlocker from the car. As I'm going back toward the dorm, she's walking past me, and I figured she'd left something in the car and was going to bring it in. I brought the footlocker to my room and I went back outside to find her. She was gone. I'm talking nothing but a memory. No kiss, no final words of encouragement. She was headed back to Gladys. That was 12 years before *Friday* was released, but that was my "Bye Felicia" moment. And it was a very scary moment. I felt like she abandoned me because I needed her support. In retrospect she was showing me tough love, or maybe it would have been too emotional for her to say goodbye. I have never asked her about it, so I'm not sure.

We went down for our first team meal, and I didn't realize that freshmen were supposed to be in the back of the line. I was up in the front. Those offensive guys, defensive guys, too, started telling me to get my ass in the back, and I said no. So they start telling me what they're going to do to me in practice. Hey, they screwed up on that one big time. I don't know what they smelled, but they didn't smell the dog that I am. I lit them up. From the moment I walked on the field, I started and dominated whoever they threw in front of me. And I was barely 175 pounds at this point.

If college was just about playing football and socializing—not to mention James Madison having a lot more girls than guys—there wouldn't have been a happier dude in Virginia. There was another aspect, though, one that became the greatest challenge of my entire life. It was obvious after my first week of taking classes that I had a ton of deficiencies, starting with reading and writing comprehension. Here I was sitting there at this prestigious academic university of higher learning and I could probably read and write at only a fifth or sixth-grade level. It was all because I was born in Gladys, where education wasn't a priority. I am certainly not without blame in this; I don't want to be

(Left) I huddle on the sideline with James Madison head coach Joe Purzycki and assistant coach Jim Pletcher. (JMU Athletics Communications)

(Right) I pressure the Virginia quarterback while in college. Playing against an ACC team was important because it brought me and Division I-AA James Madison some national attention. (JMU Athletics Communications)

(Bottom) Assistant coach Steve Wilt addresses me and a bunch of my James Madison teammates. (JMU Athletics Communications)

I drag down Cincinnati Bengals quarterback Boomer Esiason during Super Bowl XXIII, which we won 20–16. (AP Images)

(Top) Vikings offensive tackle Tim Irwin tries to block me during our 41–13 victory against Minnesota in an NFC Divisional Playoff contest at Candlestick Park. (AP Images)

(Bottom) I get in the face of Broncos quarterback John Elway during our Super Bowl XXIV beatdown against Denver. I actually felt sorry for Elway because he took such a pounding in that game. (AP Images)

Coach George Seifert talks to me during our 19–13 victory against the Atlanta Falcons in 1990. Coach and I butted heads during our time with the 49ers, but we have since mended fences. (AP Images)

(Bottom left) During a 52–14 shellacking of the Bears, I sack Chicago quarterback Jim Harbaugh, who would go on to become a successful college and NFL head coach. (AP Images) *(Bottom right) I sack Giants quarterback Phil Simms and force a fumble during our victory on December 3, 1990, but New York would get revenge and defeat us in the ensuing NFC Championship Game, preventing us from three-peating in the Super Bowl.* (AP Images)

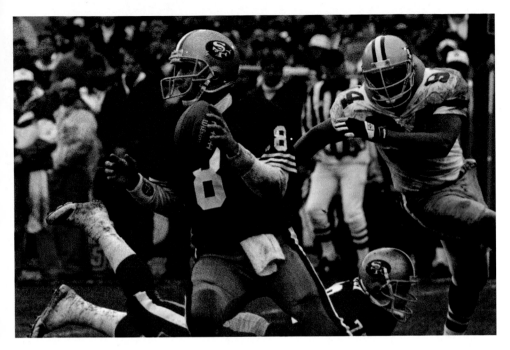

In the ultimate revenge game, I pursue 49ers quarterback Steve Young. We defeated San Francisco 30–20 in the NFC Championship Game in muddy Candlestick Park to send us to the first of our back-to-back Super Bowl appearances. (AP Images)

During my first NFC Championship Game against the San Francisco 49ers, safety James Washington and I huddle with Jimmy Johnson, who was a great coach but yelled more during that season than any other coach I ever had. (Dallas Cowboys)

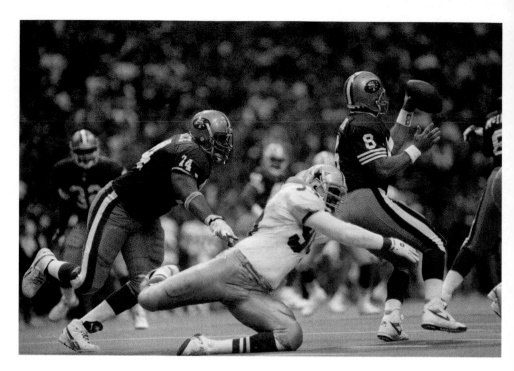

While facing the San Francisco 49ers again in the NFC Championship Game, I beat offensive tackle Steve Wallace to get to quarterback Steve Young. We won 38–21 and advanced to our second straight Super Bowl. (AP Images)

I was upset when the San Francisco 49ers beat us 38–28 in the third consecutive NFC Championship Game between the two teams. Even though we rallied late, losing to my former team represents one of the most frustrating losses of my career. (AP Images)

I tackle Green Bay running back Edgar Bennett during a victory in 1993. Along with the San Francisco 49ers, the Packers emerged as one of our rivals in the early 1990s. (Dallas Cowboys)

During our 38–10 victory over an NFC East foe in November of 1994, I go against New York Giants offensive tackle Jumbo Elliott. (Dallas Cowboys)

(Right) I pummel backup quarterback Jay Schroeder during our 38–3 beatdown of the Arizona Cardinals in 1994. (Dallas Cowboys)

(Below) In a 28–13 road win against the Atlanta Falcons, I had two sacks, including this takedown of quarterback Jeff George in 1995. (Dallas Cowboys)

that guy blaming everyone else for my own problems. Still, it was way too easy for me to float through the system.

Those last couple of years of high school, when it was obvious I could play football in college, no one helped me out in terms of preparing for the SATs or any of that stuff. The first time I took one of those tests, I just connected the dots when filling in the circles with a No. 2 pencil. I think the test was supposed to take three hours and I was finished in 10 minutes. That wasn't a good sign. Someone should have noticed that I was struggling.

I guess they were understaffed, or maybe they didn't like me, or maybe they didn't think I would amount to anything because of the poor neighborhood I was from. I'm not sure. I never went back and asked. When I left my high school, I left my high school for good. I think I went back when my nephew graduated, but that's it.

My biggest problem has always been that I have a hard time hearing words the correct way, so I would struggle to pronounce words. I couldn't hear the syllables. To this day, I really have a tough time sounding out words because of that. Other kids could sound it out and spell the word. As for me, I was sitting next to them shaking my head and failing another spelling test. I'm not sure if I was dyslexic or what. I was a slow reader and writer, but part of that problem was not knowing the words. I couldn't comprehend in the same time that others were. I needed it slowed down.

I honestly never minded school. Learning about history was interesting, and I've always been fascinated by people who changed the world like Napoleon, Abraham Lincoln, Dr. King, even an evil man like Hitler. I mean, how was this awful lunatic able to get all of these people to follow him? And I could listen to every speech Dr. King ever gave again and again.

Let's be honest, though, there was one reason I was at James Madison. That was because I played football. Now, I don't know what was going on at big-time programs then in terms of going to class or having someone write papers for the football team, but I've heard stories. At James Madison, though, academics was first, and football was second. At least that was the case under the head coach who was there my first two years. He was Challace McMillin, a soft-spoken Christian and one of the finest men I've ever had the privilege of knowing.

As I mentioned earlier, coach Danny Wilmer, the savior who found me in the middle of nowhere and recruited me to James Madison, told my mother that he would make sure I graduated. And he meant that, too. I was fortunate to come in contact with some really decent and honorable men. However, Coach McMillin was the one who truly believed I could graduate college. He had a few rules. He was by no means a stickler, but there was one set in concrete: his players would attend class. I'm talking about every class. If you skipped a class, he would find out, and there would be repercussions. He didn't care if you were an All-American, the singular most important player on the team. If you missed a class without a reason, he would sit you down without hesitation. Those first few weeks on campus, he explained to me that the school would offer whatever support, whatever extra help was needed for me to succeed in the classroom.

Know what? I've never really thought about this, but I was incredibly lucky that none of those big-time schools were smart enough to recruit me because I wouldn't have just walked on the field that first day and been the best defensive player. So I would have needed to focus more time on football. And who knows what the academic situation would have been like, if they were strict about players attending class? On every level James Madison was perfect for me.

This is important to understand: I never, ever, ever thought about playing in the NFL. Hell, I barely knew what the NFL was. I knew "Mean" Joe Greene and the names of a few teams. That was it. I knew zero about the league and/or professional football. My dream was going to college, earning a degree, having a real job that required me to think, and not having to return to Gladys.

I was not going back. I couldn't do it. All those people, teachers, coaches, guys in the neighborhood, who predicted I'd be back after hearing I was going to college, weren't going to win. I love proving those who don't believe in me wrong. I think we all do. That's what college was to me. And football gave me a chance to do that. I always tell coaches, almost every day, just give someone a chance. You never know what's going to happen.

When you're on the wrong side of the tracks in life, you don't know there's an opportunity for college. And that's not only back in my day; it's still happening. So I try to go down to those places, the worst neighborhoods in this country—the worse, the better for my message—and tell them to dream big. That's what happened to me. I dreamed big. So when I say academics were my focus more than football, that's not revisionist history. That's the absolute truth.

The first week I signed up for multiple reading and writing labs, which I wouldn't receive college credits for. There were several women there who ran the labs, and those ladies did me right. I wish I remembered their names. They were so wonderful, the most selfless teachers imaginable. After every other student had left, they spent countless hours working with me.

And I'm like a pit bull. When they told me I could go to these labs, I bit and I held onto it. I went every day. Every single day the doors were open, I was in those labs trying to catch up from a lost childhood of education.

Know what story I find myself telling a lot? The first time I went to a writing lab they had me write a paper for homework. So I come back and hand it to the woman, and she says, "Oh my God. This is... how is this possible?"

And I'm standing there like, *yeah, I wrote it, I killed it, I'm the next*

Hemingway, watch out world, here I come. The woman in this soft, kind, voice looks at me in almost disbelief and says, "This is a paper of maybe an eighth grader. How are you at James Madison?"

I yanked the paper out of her hand, ran outside, and tears started coming to my eyes. As I stopped crying, though, I realized that if I was going to stay in college, then I had to go back in there. So I walked back in, handed her the paper, and I said, "Please help me. Please help me. I don't want to fail. I can't fail."

And bless her, she did. She helped me through a lot. I spent so much more time in those labs than on the football field. That's no lie. The football team also offered us tutors, and I took advantage of those, too. I used every tool available to me academically. They taught me how to structure papers, they taught me ways to increase my reading comprehension. They taught me all those things I should have learned in high school. I stayed there during the summers to make sure I was on pace to graduate. During the season I could take three or four classes so I could dedicate myself to both football and school. I would then take two classes every summer to catch up.

I am fortunate, and this is the case to this day, in that I have a one-track mind. If I'm doing academics, that's all I think about. If I'm playing football, that's all I think about. And while I felt more comfortable at James Madison than ever before, I was hardly a social butterfly, so I didn't have many friends. I probably had two or three guys I hung around with here and there. That made it that much easier to spend almost all of my time studying or even just reading a book that wasn't assigned. The more I read, the quicker the process became. I was recognizing more and more words.

I was obsessed with turning my greatest weakness into a strength. My freshman and sophomore years, I earned almost all C's. Know what, though? I earned every damn one of them and I'm not ashamed in the least. I tell my kids all the time: from where I came from, making C's at a school like James Madison, any school really, was a big deal. Even all these years later, I have the highest regard for the professors at James Madison. Being a smaller school helped me so much. They knew all the students by name and they wanted to see you succeed. They would spend time with you after class, or you could stop by their office later in the week, and I did that all the time. Look, if there was anyone on that campus willing to spend a few minutes with me, anyone who could help me attain my goal of learning and graduating, I was all-in.

Coach McMillin, or Coach Mac as we called him, was an awesome, awesome coach. He treated all of us like we were his kids. And while he was incredibly demanding academically, there was a lot more to him. He was the first one to teach me how to break down film. I don't even remember watching film in high school. Maybe we didn't have a projector, or maybe they watched film on the days I was suspended. But Coach Mac really focused me in on watching for tendencies, habits opposing players had that could benefit me, that I could take advantage of. Over the years, especially later in my NFL career, I am guessing no defensive player watched more film than me.

He was also the first coach who taught me about visualization, how to see yourself being successful. He would talk to us about all these great things we could do, on and off the field, and how we should visualize ourselves doing them. This is something I would do for the remainder of my career. I would walk around campus thinking about being handed my diploma.

Now, so far, I've been painting quite the warm and fuzzy portrait of my college years, and that's no joke. I truly enjoyed myself, and the people I encountered changed my outlook on the world. Not everyone was out to get me. For the most part, I behaved myself, but, of course, there were some issues. Although trouble wasn't at every corner like back home, there was still just something in my brain where I almost needed to find trouble.

There was a track around our football field, and during practice I'd run players out of bounds and then launch them onto the track. For no reason either. I didn't need one. I drew some dumb penalties during games as well. There were far fewer fights than in Gladys, but there was some pushing and shoving here and there. For the most part, I was playing mind games with people, especially my teammates. I always wanted to know just how far I could push someone.

You know what I enjoy? I enjoy ripping you a new one, and then when you're ready to fight, calming you back down. My dad told me once that if I can make you laugh and I can make you cry, I control you. So it was psychology. I took a lot of psychology classes and I found more and more that I loved playing mind games. It was fun.

It wasn't long before Coach sent me to see a psychiatrist, which was actually pretty cool. She helped me relax and not be as angry with the world. I got a chance to go talk things out with her a little bit. I've spent my life going to these kinds of doctors, and some have really made an impact on me. Others are full of BS and needed a doctor more than I did.

We would spend hours in Coach's office just talking about life. Not so much football, just life. He was very proactive in my life, and without him those first years just making me believe in myself and believe that I belonged there, then I probably would have left because the next head coach that came in, Joe Purzycki, didn't care. All he cared about was winning and losing.

They fired such a good man who made sure his players were student-athletes. That's the BS they have been trying to sell us as a society all these years, right? Well, Coach Mac went 17–16 in my first three years there and graduated all of his players. The man started the football program at James Madison with a bunch of walk-ons in 1972 and ended up winning more than he lost, but that wasn't enough for what was an all-girls school 20 years before I arrived. Thing is, we went 5–6 in my last season, so the move didn't make much of a difference.

We had some talent despite being a Division I-AA program. That's a step down from the Notre Dames and Alabamas of the world, but we did beat the University of Virginia in 1982, my freshman year, and they were a Division I school. That was a big deal, a first in James Madison's history. The best player on the team that season was junior wide receiver Gary Clark, who went on to become a four-time Pro Bowl selection and two-time Super Bowl winner with the Washington Redskins. I looked up to him from a football perspective. He was great returning kicks, catching the ball. He was very determined to be the best. I watched how he carried himself. I learned a lot from him.

Speaking of UVA, before my junior year started in 1984, someone from its program came and asked me if I wanted to transfer there. They played in the prestigious Atlantic Coast Conference with Clemson, North Carolina, Maryland, and schools like that. But I would have been lost on a big campus in the world of big-time college football. I wasn't ready for any of that stuff. And those lecture classes with like 200 people in there? I wouldn't have learned a thing. As difficult academically as James Madison was, I was told Virginia was even tougher and I didn't need any more stress with the books than I was already dealing with. I stayed put.

Later that year, while I was becoming the first All-American in the program's history, I started seeing Karen, my ex-wife and the incredible mother of our four children. She was working the front desk at the Student Union, and I wrote her a poem: *Roses are red, violets are blue, if you look over here, you'll realize I love you.* I handed it to her. She was doing something else. She opened it up, read it, looked over at me, read it again, and smiled, and I knew I had her then. So that was a really great moment in my life. On our first date, we went to McDonald's.

We had known of each other for two years, seen each other around, but she was dating someone else, and I had heard that she didn't really like athletes. I was shy, too. I'm obviously very passive-aggressive and

I was more introverted in college than I am now. I still was struggling with trusting people. I didn't have many friends. James Hairston was my roommate. He was quiet, and I was quiet, so that was a good deal. I hung out with Warren Marshall, who played for the Denver Broncos, and Wayne Robinson, who went into the military, and that was more than enough friends for me.

Karen was very into her academics. She wanted to be the best, be at the top of her class. She wanted to be a lawyer. After graduating college she earned her master's degree. And that was part of my attraction to her. She helped me immensely with my schoolwork. We were always doing homework together. Karen was all about education.

It's frustrating for me, and people don't understand, but I was all about education also. They tend to roll their eyes when I say that since I made mostly C's. Let me tell you, though, I worked just as hard as anyone on the dean's list. Nothing came easy for me. There is probably nothing in our lives that Karen and I agreed on more than education, and all four of our kids graduated near the top of their classes. I am proud as hell that we were on the same page for them, no matter what else was going on.

I ended up being named the team's defensive MVP in each of my last three seasons there and an All-American as a junior and senior. They tell me I still hold the school record with 506 tackles. As a senior I was 6'4" and 200 pounds. My weight fluctuated depending on how much I was running. There were times when I was closer to 190, which is kind of crazy to think about with how much I was eating. I was burning a whole bunch of calories.

There is nothing in this great world better than an all-you-can-eat cafeteria. There would be mornings when I'd be at the door waiting for them to open it. There were lunches when I was there for two hours. I would sit there, eat a few plates, and head back up for more. When you grow up like I did, dinner could turn into a contact sport.

During my final season, nobody to my knowledge was scouting me. The only reason any NFL teams saw me was because we played UVA a few times, and they always had scouts there. And every year, I would light those dudes up. I also heard their head coach, George Welsh, told some of the scouts and coaches he knew that they needed to go across the mountain and see this linebacker. That was awfully nice of him.

So that's more or less how I was noticed. Remember, this was 1985. There was no Internet, no ESPN2, no Mel Kiper. What I didn't know until much later was that San Francisco 49ers head coach Bill Walsh was telling his staff about me during my entire senior year. He had tape and would make them watch me. He told the team's front office that they were going to draft me.

I knew none of this. The NFL wasn't in my thought process. I was hoping to graduate on time, earn my sociology degree, and maybe do some teaching and coaching. That was my plan. And if you asked me during my senior season which was more important, being drafted or graduating, I would have given you my answer in less than a second. Give me that degree.

I only had one class left that final spring, and that April was the NFL draft. I took so many credits in summer school that there was just the one class remaining. And I earned another C. There were a lot of C's on my report card. I think my GPA was around 2.4 or something like that, but let me tell you this: aside from the birth of my four children, graduating from James Madison is the biggest and greatest highlight of my life. It's more important than the five Super Bowls, the Hall of Fame, whatever. That degree let my family, everyone in Gladys, everyone at James Madison—who must have been wondering how this guy ended up here—know that all you need in life is a dream and an opportunity.

That's what this world is all about. First you need the dream, and mine was an education. Second, I needed the opportunity, and football allowed me to attend a great school. They said I was from the wrong side of the street for that sort of dream, that sort of opportunity. There were a lot of young men who were every bit the football player I was but who didn't have the opportunity or didn't take advantage of their opportunity. That wasn't going to be me.

There were many mornings at James Madison when I was in those reading and writing labs before and after my classes. Then I went to practice and back to the labs. Maybe I was going to flunk out because I wasn't smart enough, but it wasn't going to be from a lack of trying.

You can't be scared of failure. There ain't nothing wrong with failing. It's part of life. I've failed many times. There's only something wrong with never giving yourself the chance to fail. It often takes courage to fail.

I tell groups I talk with now, especially kids, younger players, that everything comes in steps. There's nothing wrong with having a goal at the top of the steps, but don't overlook the journey there. Pay attention in school, read and write at every opportunity, get the best education you can in high school, and somehow, someway, get into college. Junior college, four-year, whatever, just find a way, and then dedicate yourself to earning that degree. Whatever happens after that is that, but if you have your base, you are all set. Sure, there's still going to be ups and downs, but if you have that education, you can adapt, you can succeed. You're not going to be living in a trailer in Gladys.

I owe James Madison a ton. I've tried to pay them back by bringing positive publicity to the college. I have nothing but love for them. They ended up inducting me to the school's athletic Hall of Fame, which was a real thrill. And Coaches Mac and Wilmer were there. I showed up struggling to read and write and left with a degree. That's the American Dream right there.

The 49ers came and visited me at school. I did run the 40-yard dash in 4.49 seconds, but I only bench pressed 225 pounds two times. That's the weight they have the players do at the NFL Scouting Combine to this day, and a Dallas Cowboys kicker did it 25 times a few years back. I never lifted weights. It wasn't my thing. I ran, did drills, and watched film, but the weights, not so much. I was country strong, my legs were strong, and I'd be there on gameday.

One of the coaches gave me $50 and told me to take my girl out to eat, so Karen and I had a nice dinner. That was my pre-draft experience. Well, the New York Giants flew me up there. That was the first time I had ever flown, and they brought me to their headquarters. I lifted and then they took me back to the airport. No one talked to me. There was no interview. I was there for like 20 minutes.

I never heard from anyone else. Heck, I barely heard from the 49ers and the Giants. I just figured I wasn't good enough, which had always been my mind-set anyway. My brothers were born doing everything great, and then there was Charles, tripping over his own feet, the class clown, the clown in general. Why would any NFL team have an interest in me? This was my thought process.

A few folks were telling me I was going in the second or third round, but I had no idea. There were like 12 rounds back then. Karen and I went down to the movies on a bicycle. I was peddling; she was sidesaddle. It must've been April 29, 1986. I have no idea what movie was playing. My roommate came running into the theater and told me the 49ers had just drafted me. He literally ran there. It was just down the hill from campus, and he was so excited. He was breathing heavy when he told me they were on the phone. He said they wanted me to call them back. I didn't know whether or not he was doing a prank, so we stayed and finished the movie.

It wasn't a prank. They took me in the fourth round with the 96th overall selection. They told me to take a plane out there. They had booked the flight and all that. So I flew from Harrisonburg, Virginia, to Dulles Airport in Washington, D.C., to San Francisco. This was my first time in a big city by myself. I walk off the plane, and there was no one at the gate when we landed, so I asked this white guy where the baggage claim was. He turned to me and started speaking another language. I found a black dude and asked him, and he starts speaking another language. I was scared out of my mind. I really wanted to go back to the gate and ask the pilot to take me back home. I'm honestly not sure I have ever been that scared. I'd never met people that spoke different languages before, and it was frightening. It was a frightening experience for a country boy like me.

At that point a man walked up to me and said he was there to take me to the team headquarters and that he was running a little late. It was Jon Gruden, who later won a Super Bowl as the head coach of the Tampa Bay Buccaneers and is now the television analyst for *Monday Night Football*. He was an entry-level errand boy at the time. That's when the magic started. He mentioned on the ride there how excited I must be to be playing for Bill Walsh and with Joe Montana and Ronnie Lott. I asked him, "Who are they?"

Chapter 4

Welcome to the NFL

I'M 100 PERCENT SERIOUS. I had absolutely no clue who these NFL coaches and players were when I was drafted. I had never watched a Super Bowl, never mind a regular-season NFL game. I knew the folks in my neighborhood back home in Gladys, I knew Elmer Fudd and Yosemite Sam, I knew the Jackson 5, and I knew just about everyone at James Madison. I'm pretty sure Bill Walsh or Roger Craig weren't to be found in any of the aforementioned.

It almost goes without saying then that I wasn't in awe of my new teammates. It's tough to be in awe of the unknown. And you know what? Looking back, that certainly helped me. It made me feel like I belonged, whereas a lot of kids from smaller schools probably would have gone in there intimidated and wide-eyed.

Being drafted was a joyful moment for my family and me, but it was also a sad time because the agent I went with on the advice of my college roommate ended up signing some documents in my name and took out a bunch of money from some banks. It's a shady business, and obviously I was oblivious to that.

Fortunately, I had Karen, and she saved me. We weren't married yet—Karen was finishing up her master's degree during my rookie season, so we were married that following offseason—but I showed her all of the documents, and she said to not sign anything. We drove down to where the agent was in Southern Virginia and we went to every bank and explained that we didn't want any loans and that I hadn't seen a dollar from the money already taken out. The banks were able to get most of the money back from the agent, and I wasn't held accountable for any of it. I, of course, fired the agent.

I always had trust issues to begin with. I'm sure that's obvious by this point, and this didn't help. In my head every time I tried to do something good for someone, it backfired. My college roommate recommended the agent, so I didn't like him much anymore after that. The entire episode left a bad taste in my mouth, especially for agents, but thank God, like so many other times, Karen was there to save me.

I ended up signing that first year for a $60,000 signing bonus and a $70,000 base contract. I know that doesn't sound like much nowadays when spare-ass third-stringers are making a couple of million, but this was the spring of 1986, and for me this was crazy dough. I'm not sure I ever had more than $100 in my pocket.

I also knew, and was often reminded by Karen, that we never knew when my football career could end, so we weren't going to be those idiots buying blinged-out jewelry or diamond-studded rims. Yeah, just what we all need, right? The first thing I bought was a Toyota pickup truck mostly because I had some dogs—I've always had a few dogs, even to this very day—and it was supposed to be a reliable car. And it was. That lasted me a long time. I've never been a flashy guy. I never wear jewelry, even though I have some from gifts over the years. It's just not the way I am.

I remember calling my mother after signing the contract and telling her the numbers, and she started screaming, "We hit the lotto! We hit the lotto!" She was so excited. After a few minutes, though, she told me not to screw it up. She reminded me that there were no rooms around her house. I remember to this day her saying, "This is why you went to college. So you never have to come back here."

That probably sounds like excessive tough love, but I always understood her message. She read me the riot act every chance she had, but that's what I needed. She knew how to make a point. Looking back, my mother is a lot like Karen. They are authoritarian; they take charge. Whereas, much like my father, I'm more passive. Not on the field or in the locker room, just in life in general. I was always fine with

Karen making the decisions for us. "Hey, whatever you want, honey. I'm going to watch Bugs Bunny or take the kids to the playground." I was a totally different guy in the locker room and on the field, where I ran things. When I came home, I didn't try to run things. I let Karen do what she wanted. I basically married my momma.

I was running that entire spring, and by the time of my first weigh-in, I was barely 200 pounds. Imagine that today, a pass rusher at 200 pounds! Most wide receivers are more than that.

The team told me to go home and gain some weight, to at least get up to 225 pounds. I tried, I tried, I tried. I ate everything humanly possible, but as an athlete, you've got to feel good about where you are weight-wise in order to be productive, so I didn't stay at 225. Usually they fine you for being underweight or overweight, but they gave me latitude and longitude throughout my career. I wanted to be big and strong. That sounded great in theory, but I didn't like lifting and I loved running.

I never had a six-pack stomach. Hell, I never had a two-pack—like ever. Not high school, not college, and certainly not in the NFL. That stuff didn't matter to me. All of these guys that walk around looking like Tarzan, and then they play like Jane. I'd rather look like Jane and play like Tarzan. That was my deal. Luckily, Coach Walsh was one of those coaches who didn't believe in lifting weights, and I was good with that. They ran us ragged, but I loved those coaches for that. I loved running, doing football drills, practicing. That was my thing.

No one was going to outwork me; that was my promise to myself that first season. That's easy to say but a whole lot tougher to prove. When there's just a coach and a player on the practice field day after day, though, that's how you walk the walk. Once I arrived at the team facility, I met with assistant coach Tommy Hart, who worked with the defensive linemen. He played 13 years in the NFL, mostly with San Francisco as a defensive end, and was selected to the Pro Bowl in 1976.

We talked a little bit, and I told him that I wanted to contribute from the first day of training camp, so he said we would work out for an hour a day every day for the two months before then.

We did mostly pass rush stuff. He showed me all the tricks in the book. I love that man to death. On most days the hour quickly turned into two or three, and then we would watch film together. I was picking the stuff up so quickly. For whatever reason, while I needed some extra time and help with stuff like math and science, watching football film or reading a playbook came rather easy to me. It became like second nature to me.

One time we were out there and instead of hitting the tackling dummy, I accidently hit his shoulder and hit him upside the head. Coach Hart said, "Let me show you how to do that move." He came over. I had my helmet off, and he's standing there in a T-shirt and shorts. He came up, hit my shoulder, hit my head, and knocked my ass to the ground. That man was strong. He literally took me off my feet and put me on the ground. I made sure to never miss the tackling dummy and hit Coach Hart again.

I was learning so much every day. It was stimuli overload. Those two months were the foundation for my success in the NFL. I was so fortunate that Coach Hart took the time to work with me and to understand me. We all know I can be difficult, but I recall that being one of the happiest times of my life. It was just him and me on that field.

After our workouts I'd run some sprints, shower, and then watch film. I would try and pick something up from every great pass rusher the team had on tape. I'd watch Lawrence Taylor for hours, day after day. He was similar to me in terms of using technique and speed rather than brute strength. To me he's the greatest pass rusher to ever live.

A few years later, when I was named to my first Pro Bowl in 1988, I bought drinks for L.T. for hours down at the beach in front of our hotel, and trust me, I'm not one to easily pick up the tab. You know what they say about rich people: they stay rich by not spending money. But I wanted to hear every secret these all-time greats possessed.

Since Reggie White didn't drink, Reggie and I would hang out back at the hotel. With Reggie, he wanted to talk with me about God first, which was cool, but after that, he'd start showing me some stuff. I wish I had paid even more attention to every word he said. Reggie was a really good man, and it was devastating that he died so young at just 43 years old in 2004.

Reggie taught me the "hump" move, which was exploding out of your position, forcing the offensive lineman to commit, then crossing in front of him, and hitting him with your arm across the shoulder pads. He was telling me the move was about power, but I countered that it was actually about leverage. I used it in a game, threw the guy off me, tallied a sack, and, sure enough, tore my rotator cuff in the process. So I learned to never argue with the guys on that Mount Rushmore. They know their stuff. I also learned that it's about power; it ain't about no daggum leverage.

My studying of other pass rushers continued throughout my career, no matter how many Super Bowls or Pro Bowls I was named to. I wanted to see what the top-tier pass rushers were doing. Maybe one of them came up with a new move. Maybe one added a tweak to their technique that would allow me to find the quarterback a nanosecond quicker. I was looking for any advantage. I would sit there for hours in a dark room watching film of Bruce Smith, Pat Swilling, Derrick Thomas. The video guys would make cut-ups after cut-ups for me, and I would sit there taking notes. I wanted to know what every pass rusher in the league was doing. If a dude had one career sack in the NFL, I wanted to see that sack on tape.

I felt pretty confident at the first minicamp even before Coach Hart and I went through our own football boot camp, but the real difference, the fruits of our labor, was showcased in the first few practices of training camp. I was so fast, so quick off the ball that none of the tackles could block me. That definitely boosted my confidence because iron sharpened iron. Those guys had been starting for years, and this was a team just two seasons removed from finishing 15–1 en route to winning their second Super Bowl title in four years. This was the best of the best.

Those offensive linemen, guys like Randy Cross and Bubba Paris, were known as brilliant technicians. And there I was, whooping their ass. That definitely helped me. My motto then and throughout my career was "by any means necessary" because I didn't want to go back home as anything but a success.

That first season, like I am guessing it is for most players, was a whirlwind. There was so much happening, so many new experiences. For the most part, my teammates accepted me. There was the typical rookie stuff, but in the end, looking back—Joe Montana, Ronnie Lott, Jerry Rice, the stars of the team—all introduced themselves to me and accepted me as one of them, one of the group. I never felt ostracized.

For being the greatest quarterback to ever walk this planet, Joe was a trip. He was always chill, too, which was probably his greatest attribute on the field. He was definitely "Joe Cool." Here's a guy who won four Super Bowls, was a first-ballot Hall of Fame inductee, was widely thought of as the best, and he liked a practical joke as much as anyone. Joe was always one of the guys.

He would put talcum powder in your jock. He would put cream of Jesus in your jock. He would get there early, early in the morning and he would put your bicycle up in the treetops. That was one of his favorites. He would take the seat off so that the spike would be there with no pad, no place to sit. And he'd be laughing all the time. Boy, was he a jokester, one of the all-time pranksters. We talked so much trash, me and him. I used to call him Barry Manilow because of his big nose. I used to call him Pinocchio. Joe would call me Bullet Head. During one practice I started yelling, "Coach, coach, stop the play! Joe's offside. His nose is across the ball," and everybody just started laughing.

I remember when Joe's wife, Jennifer, went into labor, I grabbed the loudspeaker for the locker room and said, "Hey, everyone, let me have your attention. Big news. Jennifer went to the hospital today and delivered a seven-pound, three-ounce nose."

And let me tell you, there will be no doubt today, tomorrow, and forever: Joe Montana is the best damn quarterback I've ever seen. That guy pulled wins out of the deepest depths of defeat, and I'm pretty sure he did so without his pulse or heart rate increasing a beat. Other guys are shitting their jock in Week 1 of the preseason.

Earlier I was talking about how no one was going to outwork me. That sounded all well and good until I met Jerry Rice. That man could run circles around me and then he would keep on running. There's a reason he owns all of the league's receiving records. That dude was crazy. I'm sure everyone has seen the clips of him running the hills of San Francisco. That dude was outrunning the trolleys.

I went with him to train one time. We went to this little college, I forget the name of it, and we were just running down the field and back. I was in pretty good shape, the best shape of my life, and I was about done, literally exhausted. But Rice looks at me and says, all serious, "I think that's good for the warm-up." He was for real. No kidding around. This dude was literally just doing his warm-up. I grabbed my water bottle, found the nearest tree, and took my cleats off. And as he kept running around and doing all of these drills, I got in my car and went home. I told him I was never coming back and I never did. Damn, I'm shaking my head just thinking about it 30 years later.

Then there was Ronnie Lott. I have no idea why to this day, but Ronnie immediately took a liking to me. He would take me to George Chung's martial arts training, and I learned how to use my hands and feet quickly and how to be able to keep my eyes open and focused when people were punching and hitting my face. That was profound for me. Doing hand moves and using leverage, unbalancing people took me to another level. I could unbalance linemen and then just throw them aside. They could be as strong as a bull, and I'd throw them with one hand. And I'm a guy who never lifted weights in his life. Football isn't all about muscles. Heck, you should have seen Joe in the locker room.

And while the martial arts definitely helped me, just being around Ronnie had such a positive impact on me as well. I trust Ronnie with my life. I did then and I do now. That for me was pretty big. At the time, I could count on a single hand how many people I trusted. By the time I came into the league, Ronnie was a perennial Pro Bowler, an All-Pro, but he was only four years older than me. A natural leader, respected by everyone in the locker room on both offense and defense, Ronnie was the guy we all wanted to be like and carry ourselves like.

Ronnie did a ton of charity stuff and early in my rookie season he grabbed me by the ear and made me come along. We were giving out shoes at this barbershop, and I remember parents coming up crying, thanking us so much. From that day on, all he had to do was ask me. Now my whole life has been built around giving back because of him and that day.

I grew up helping the elderly and the sick through the church and my mother's instruction, of course. But as you start going through life and become an adult, you start thinking you're too big for your britches and you forget about those people, you know? Ronnie brought me back down to earth pretty quickly, and even though I developed the reputation as the big, bad Charles Haley, the media guys and cameras weren't around when I was doing outreach work almost every week during my career. And I liked it that way. I wasn't helping or offering my time and/or money for any reason other than I wanted to make someone's life better.

Over the years to come, Ronnie would stick his head into a hornet's nest a whole bunch of times for me. I was never looking for friends, but I was lucky enough to find one for life in Ronnie. He's going to hate me for saying this, but Ronnie was really my guardian angel.

It's really amazing to think about this assembled talent in one place at one time. I'm 100 percent behind the idea that when I was drafted by the 49ers they featured the greatest quarterback, wide receiver, safety, and head coach—all in their primes—in the nearly 100 years of the NFL. Unreal. For a team to have just two of those would be unthinkable.

Now, just because I was treated decently as a rookie doesn't mean I avoided hazing, which back then was more or less mandatory. These days rookies have to bring donuts and maybe get their heads shaved at camp. It was a little rougher in my day. And I'm sure other rookies have stories about some of the stuff I put them through later in my career.

I did it all as a rookie, though. I carried the film projector to every which room they told me. After we finished up watching film one day, long after practice when it was time to go home, the offensive and defensive linemen picked me up and carried me outside to the field. This wasn't going to end well, I knew that.

They taped my hands behind my back, taped my feet around the goal post, even taped my head to the post. They were taking no chances. And at that point, they put a jock in my mouth. I'm still trying to fig-ure out whether it was dirty or clean. Or maybe I don't want to know. If it weren't for Bill Walsh looking outside his office window and tell-ing somebody to go cut me down, I probably would have been out there until the next day. They did all kinds of stuff like that to me.

Also during my rookie season, we did this event in Pittsburg, which is up in the mountains near San Francisco. It was an annual outing for kids, and most of the rookies went. The night before I had been drinking and I hit the guardrail with my car while going around a curve. No one was hurt, but I was petrified. I felt horrible.

So we're driving back from the event, we were all in a van, and a police officer pulls us over. As he approaches the window, he says, "Is Charles Haley here?" I walk up the aisle of the van, and the police officer says, "We have a warrant out for a hit-and-run last night." So they take me out of the van and handcuff me. I've been in some trouble before, but I had never been handcuffed. That was something else. I'm in the back of the squad car, and my life is finished.

Then we walk into the police station, and they take the cuffs off. However, a few seconds later, the police chief walks out and starts screaming about me not being in handcuffs and he throws me against the wall. I was scared beyond shitless.

Then everyone starts busting out laughing.

The guys had set that up as a little practical joke. And everybody thought it was okay to do crap like that to me. For me, it was just too much. It's the worst type of humor, and I always figured the worst was going to happen.

The ones pulling most of the pranks were linebacker Keena Turner, cornerback Eric Wright, Joe, and nose tackle Michael Carter. And "Big Mike" was usually the ringleader. The thing about Mike was that nobody messed with him, and, really, no one talked to him. When I came in, though, I don't care if you're the president or the shoe-shine boy, I'm going to treat everyone the same, so I was always messing around with Mike, who was a big boy, like 300 pounds, and a heck of a player. He was a three-time Pro Bowl selection.

One day I was messing with Mike—my locker was right beside his—and he was taping his hand. I'm grabbing him, just trying to annoy him, and he hits me in the chest. I mean, he hit me, and I went flying back until my ass hit the back of my locker and I collapsed. I jumped up and I'm looking at that dog because I'm ready to fight now.

And standing there, looking at Mike, I decided, you know what, I want no part of that one and I sat my ass right back down.

I grew to love Mike. He was one of my favorite teammates, though definitely a man of few words, but we were always good after that. He would invite my family over to eat and hang out. He was a big family guy, and that was something really positive for me, having someone reach out like that.

For the most part, though, once I made the team, the locker room became like a frat house where we did all kinds of practical jokes. You sit there and you say all kinds of things about each other. It was just a free-for-all. A team that laughs together plays together and sacrifices together, and we did that.

When it was time for practice, I was lights out, 100 percent. When I walk out there, they better stretch because I'm coming and I was that way because of my love and respect for the game. That drove me to new levels and new heights. I wanted to be the best. I wanted to be like Ronnie and Joe. I wanted to be known as the best pass rusher in the NFL.

The last preseason game of my rookie season, while playing special teams—I think we were playing the Seattle Seahawks—I was knocked out cold. I ran through the wedge on a kickoff and made the tackle, and that was that, lights out, sleepy time. The first thing I heard when I came to was Coach Walsh telling the special teams coach, "As long as I'm the head coach of the 49ers, Charles won't be playing any more special teams—not a single down."

I'll talk more about concussions and injuries in another chapter, but yeah, that was the first of many times I was knocked out. That happened a bunch. I don't remember much from that first time. I think I walked off the field, but I honesty don't remember. I could have been carried off. That happened a few times. And this isn't me forgetting the specifics 30 years later. I didn't remember the 10 or 15 minutes after the hit on the day it took place.

The rest of my rookie season was a bunch of headaches. Ask me about my rookie season, and that's my first memory—the headaches. At our team facility, they took this little office that the doctors had and turned it into a room where I could go during the week. I was having such chronic head pain that they put these dark, black glasses on me, turned off all the lights, and I'd sit in this vibrating chair and listen to music. This would relax me and help with the headaches so I could play. That was every week of that first season.

I don't remember much, but I remember the pain of those headaches like it was 30 seconds ago. I didn't practice much that first year because of the migraines. I spent more time in that room with dark glasses on than I did on the practice field, which made the work I put in with Coach Hart that spring all the more valuable and necessary.

My rookie season also offered me one of my most important lessons, that being you're better off not talking to the media. As you can imagine, there wasn't a lot of reporters in Gladys or even at James Madison. And by a lot, I mean any. Maybe some guy from the school paper asked me a question here and there, but they were on the same team as me and weren't trying to make me look bad or twist my words.

The print media can write whatever they want. You can say, "Hold on, I was misquoted, I didn't say that," but the information, the words are already out there. Everyone has already read them. Our minds have moved on. It's like when someone is accused of a murder or any crime and it's on the front page of the newspaper for three days. When they are found not guilty or it ends up that they aren't even charged, the news is buried on the back of the comics.

I gave a story to a guy during my rookie year, answered all of his questions, couldn't have been nicer. The next day I read it, and he made me look like an idiot. And honestly, I wasn't much of a conversationalist at the time. Most of my answers were just yes, no, I kept it pretty simple. So how the hell could he have this big-ass feature story on me anyhow? He had like three and four-sentence quotes from me. I didn't give three or four-sentence answers to my mother or Karen or Coach Walsh. I sure as hell wasn't giving them to some stranger with ketchup stains on his shirt.

Then the jackass has all of these quotes from anonymous sources saying I was Dr. Jekyll and Mr. Hyde, and no one knows what to expect from Charles. Well, guess what? Here's what you can expect from Charles going forward: no answers. Nothing. You're going to write what you want anyway, so why do I need to talk? And that was it. My experience with the media thereafter was a whole lot of "no comment" and "get out of my face, asshole."

That first season I somehow played in all 16 games coming off the bench and led the team with 12 sacks and four forced fumbles. We lost our first playoff game, though, and in San Francisco, you are judged by winning the Super Bowl. Instead, we lost to the New York Giants 49–3. That sucked. And we lost our first playoff game again the following year. After that, my teams won 14 of their next 15 playoff games.

Over time, the memories of specific plays and games fade more and more. What remains are the relationships, the people, the friends. That's why I have so many regrets today because I should have treated my teammates and coaches better. There is one man, though, that I have no regrets about how I treated, and that's Bill Walsh, my head coach those first three years with San Francisco. I loved that man so much. I was in awe of him. And for whatever reason, he treated me as well as anyone ever has—before or since. The most brilliant football coach we have ever seen, winner of three Super Bowls, treated me as an equal, as a man, as a son.

The very first time we spoke, he shook my hand, and we started talking about football. He knew I could be sensitive, so he told the other coaches not to piss me off. I don't recall George Seifert, who was the defensive coordinator those first three years before becoming my head coach, even talking to me when Bill was there.

The defensive coaches knew I knew the playbook as well as they did. I could tell you what every single player on the field was supposed to do—on offense and defense. I would attend quarterback meetings, offensive line meetings. The position coaches would be like, "Charles, don't you have your own meeting to attend?" And I'd be like, "I know everything from that meeting. I want to learn something new, and Coach Walsh said it was okay."

Another aspect of Bill that I loved was that when he spoke to me we weren't having long discussions, so nothing was lost in communication. I had some issues where if someone talked to me for too long, say more than 30 seconds, all I took from it was the negative. I wasn't hearing the positive stuff because once I heard a single negative word, real or imagined, my mind was off and running. Bill understood that. He told me a few times that criticism was like beef jerky. It's tough, it's hard to chew, but it has everything you need in it if you choose to use it. The first time he said that to me, he paused for a second and added, "And you should choose to use it, Charles." I always thought that was funny. It makes me laugh to this day.

Know what else? I never heard Bill Walsh raise his voice. Not once. Not during some BS pregame pep talk, not in anger, heck, not even at me. And I pissed everyone off. I have so many lasting memories of Bill. I got in trouble once—well, more than once—and I'm talking to him on the practice field. I said, "Coach, why don't you just tell me what to do?" That's what I was used to, coaches just telling me what to do. And he smiled and said, "You have never asked me that before." So I dropped my head like the lecture is coming and nothing, not a word. I look up and he's 20 yards away, walking downfield. I yelled, "That's all I have to do?" And he nods his head yes. He never gave any actual instruction, but I just thought it was cool how there was such mutual respect between us.

From then on, we took our relationship to another level. I was never afraid to ask for help. I never wanted those consequences of being in trouble or letting him down, so I tried to behave myself, at least as best as I could. Honestly, I never thought I would have that kind of a relationship with anybody because, well, for the most part, no one talked to me like that. I mean, I could BS and be the class clown, make people laugh, but no one was having meaningful conversations with me.

Coach Walsh would call me up to his office and say about five words. At the beginning of my third season, in 1988, he called me in and said, "The starting job is yours. It's yours to lose, now get out." And he smiled. I love that. Short, simple, to the point. Don't confuse me; don't piss me off. Nothing is missed. No chance for my mind to start racing. Some dude might be telling me how great I am, but I'm thinking about someone making fun of me growing up, and after a few minutes, I'm pissed at this poor dude who is being nice to me.

My biggest downfall is that I always remember everything anyone has ever done to me, I mean my entire life. Yet for whatever reason, I don't remember what I did to them. That makes for difficult relationships. Bill understood me in ways I didn't even fully appreciate. Back when I was playing for him, I saw him once on television mention my bipolar disorder, that I had more going on than anyone realized. This was like 15 years before I was officially diagnosed, but he knew. No one on the team ever asked me about it, but they obviously had some idea about what was going on. I even sometimes wonder if they were giving me medication during the season, telling me they were vitamin supplements or something, you know? Was it to keep my bipolar under control? Especially when Bill was there, I was mostly under control.

Coach was so ahead of his time, not only as an offensive genius, but off the field, too. He sent all of his rookies to see a psychologist on Tuesdays. We had no choice. And yeah, I was annoyed. I was annoyed because I wanted to be home, especially when Karen was in town.

Hell, I wanted to be anywhere in the world besides talking to a doctor about my issues.

I went in there one day with a bad attitude, all messed up. I ended up telling her about how life was back home in Gladys, about young boys and what we did with farm animals. As I'm hitting my stride, I jumped up from the couch screaming, and the poor lady doctor, she flipped over in her chair. And before she even stands up, she says, "You don't have to come anymore, I promise. I'll take care of it." I scared the crap out of her. I guess she just handled my evaluation from that last meeting. Coach Walsh never made me go back. And for the record, yeah, I was joking about the farm animals.

Bill was there for all of his players. He wanted to take care of all of us. It wasn't just me. He never told people what to do either. He surrounded himself with leaders—both coaches and players. Ronnie, Keena, Eric, Joe, Jerry, those guys led us. He wanted leaders on his football teams, which wasn't an accident. Know what he always told us? He would say, "You have to overcome your coaching." I loved that one. You have to overcome your coaching, and this was from Bill *freaking* Walsh. I think the world of him.

And Bill was always bringing people in to talk with us, especially during training camp. There were boxers who had just won a championship, gold medal-winning figure skaters, baseball and basketball players, best-selling authors, actors, whoever had a story to tell us about how they rose to the top of their profession, how they became great. Instead of standing up there himself and telling us, which most coaches do, Bill brought in these people with incredible success stories to talk with us. I thought that was pretty cool. I appreciated that.

That first preseason, Bill comes walking in the locker room with this newspaper that wrote that we were in a rebuilding mode. He was not happy. He was throwing the paper around the room and saying, "Did you see this? They think we're rebuilding, and you're done," and then he threw it at our feet. Then he would read another paragraph and throw another paper. He must have staged this all out in his mind before walking in. He had like 10 copies of the paper, but I was on the edge of my seat. He said, and this is really the attitude I played with my entire career, every season, every game: "I don't know what the hell they are talking about. We are built to win now. I never knew that you're supposed to do anything but win. Anyone that thinks we're rebuilding can leave now."

There was never any rebuilding in Bill's mind. And I can promise you there was no rebuilding if I was around. There are two people in this world I have always listened to: my mother and Bill Walsh. I honestly think Bill was the greatest orator I ever heard in my life.

Bill coached me for three years with the 49ers before he stepped down. People tell me I should just be thankful for that time, and I am. I think about him all the time, every day.

For a guy to know me for a few years and then decide to commit himself to the rest of my life, I'd never had anybody do that before. He did a lot for me. I don't know why he liked me. I have never figured that part out. I was probably a pain in his ass, but he loved me anyway.

Throughout my career, Bill was always there. He would call me from time to time. When I had a problem, Bill was one of my first phone calls. When my career ended, he called and said, "What do you want? What do you want to do now? How can I help you?" And whatever I said, whatever my answers were, he would make a phone call and make it happen. That's how he impacted my life.

Coach Walsh passed away from leukemia on July 30, 2007. Two days before that, he called me. After we exchanged pleasantries, he said, "What can I do for you Charles? How can I help?" I said, "Coach, how can I help you? I can come out and spend some time with you, visit," and he said softly, "I'm not doing the chemo anymore. I just can't."

We talked for a few minutes and two days later, he passed. He was gone. I miss him so much. As I've grown as a man, as I've overcome my demons, I want my coach to be able to see the man he helped shape. I wanted him there when I was inducted to the Pro Football Hall of Fame. I wanted him to present me. I just want to talk with him.

I didn't attend his funeral because, well, you know what, I still see Coach Walsh every day. In my thoughts, in my dreams, in my hopes to improve as a man each day, I still see Coach Walsh. And I didn't want to see him lying in a casket. I didn't want to see the finality of him dying. I still see him being a joy of light, just bouncing around, drawing up plays on the chalkboard, and telling me to get out of his office with that smile of his. And he told some funny jokes, too.

Anyway, that's what I see. I see the man I love so much. I don't want to see that vision of him lying in a coffin. He's not dead to me. He'll forever live in my mind and heart. And I'll spend my life until my dying moments trying to spread the wisdom and class he taught me.

Chapter 5

Self-Destruction

THE FINAL TIME that Bill Walsh coached an NFL game was on January 22, 1989, at Joe Robbie Stadium in Miami Gardens, Florida. It was Super Bowl XXIII, and we were playing the Cincinnati Bengals. Some think it's the greatest Super Bowl ever played, and it might have been. Without question it was the best one I was ever involved in. And not just because it was my first one either.

All that craziness during the week, everyone wanting tickets, partying, and whatnot, I didn't experience any of that in Miami. I was named to my first Pro Bowl that year, but I wasn't a well-known guy, especially with all of the star power we had. That was fine by me. I didn't have many friends and I wasn't trying to make any more. My parents came, and I had two kids by then, so Karen brought my son and daughter, and that was about it. The guys I grew up with, my college teammates, every Tom, Dick, and Harry I met along the way, they didn't have my number, and I wasn't giving it out anyhow.

Since my first day with the team, Coach Walsh was always saying, "Champions behave like champions before they are champions." And this was our chance to prove it. We didn't exactly dominate the competition that season, going just 6–5 in our first 11 games before we started rolling and won four of our last five. We then defeated the Minnesota Vikings and Chicago Bears in the playoffs by a combined 50 points, so we definitely peaked at the right time.

The big story that week in Miami wasn't Joe Montana or Bill Walsh or Bengals quarterback Boomer Esiason. Nope, the story was Cincinnati's rookie running back Ickey Woods and that "Ickey Shuffle" dance he did after touchdowns. He was just a rookie, and boy, let me tell you, he was a blazing back, just explosive. I was really impressed watching him on film.

Ronnie Lott laid the hit of the game on him. He came up from his safety position, and in one of those moments in time where it's all slow motion, just hit Ickey, and he kind of fell backward like a tree. He hurt his knee in the second game of the following season and was never the same, but I always thought the beginning of the end for his career was that hit Ronnie gave him, which really changed the momentum of the Super Bowl for us.

My biggest memory, beside the outcome, was going up against Bengals left tackle Anthony Munoz all day. This man is one of the best to ever play offensive line. Some say he's the gold standard. I wouldn't argue that. I finished the game with two sacks, but I promise you every play was an exhaustive battle of wills. I have a ton of respect for Munoz, a fellow Pro Football Hall of Famer. I think he and former Rams tackle Jackie Slater were the two greatest offensive linemen during my time in the league.

Slater hit me so hard once that I saw Jesus Christ in all three forms. And after Slater did, he waved his finger at me like I'm a little kid. It was like, "I wouldn't try that one again if I were you because I just flipped your ass." I had tried running over the top of him. I've made some mistakes in my life, but that one ranks right up there. So I left the game after that hit and I went way down on the bench where the kickers were chilling. I sat down there and I tossed my helmet aside. I was contemplating whether I wanted to play this damn game ever again. I was thinking I should have been a farmer.

As I was pondering my future, my position coach, Bill McPherson —a good guy who we called Coach Mac—comes over and says, "You better get your ass back in the game or you're going to be on the next bus to Gladys." So I went back in the game. I didn't want to go over to the side with Jackie, and neither did our other defensive end, Larry Roberts. Both of us lined up on the opposite side. I have no idea how the quarterback didn't see this. If they had just run to Jackie's side, they could have scored with Rerun from that show, *What's Happening!!*, carrying the ball.

Instead, quarterback Jim Everett dropped back to pass, and I came off the corner unblocked and got a sack. That built my confidence up, so I went back to Jackie's side. My plan going forward was to take a step out and just try running around him. I never wanted any physical contact with the man again. I was all for bringing some physicality to my game, just not so much with Jackie.

Anyhow, the Super Bowl against the Bengals was a close, hard-fought game. Neither team ever led by more than a score. They returned a kickoff for a touchdown in the third quarter and took a 16–13 lead late in the fourth on a field goal. I sat down on the bench and started crying. There was like three minutes left, and we were on our own 8-yard line. I was basically shaking my fist at God, asking, "Why did you bring me here to lose?" Like Coach Walsh told us, "The only yardstick for success is being a champion," and I wanted to be a champion to show all of those people who had called me a bum. I wanted to show them who I really was. So there I was on the bench with my head in my hands. I was crying, sobbing, feeling like this was my fault, that I could have done more. Then I started hearing the cheers. That was me forgetting who my teammates were. That was me forgetting who my head coach was.

Of course, like I should have expected, Joe Montana was Joe, completing passes to Roger Craig and Jerry Rice like they were the only players on the field. Then finally, with the world expecting him to throw to Jerry, Joe finds John Taylor in the end zone for the winning touchdown. That's why he's the greatest quarterback ever. There is no debate in my mind. We won the game 20–16.

The lesson I learned from that is to believe in my teammates 100 percent, and I never doubted my teammates again. I never gave up on a game again. I never doubted that we couldn't win from that point on, no matter how dire the situation. That drive, that win, that game strengthened my resolve because I took the coward's way out by assuming we were going to lose. And, honestly, I was riding their coattails the entire season. Being able to play on that kind of team, the last one coached by Bill Walsh, that's one of the great honors of my life.

Winning a Super Bowl changes who you are as a football player. It just does, and I'm pretty sure everyone who has won a championship would agree. It's the respect from all of the other players and people in the league. They would come up to you, pat you on the back, and be like, "Yeah man, you got this. I wish I could win one." That was the biggest thing for me. Once you win a Super Bowl, you're a champion. The rest of your life, you are Super Bowl champion Charles Haley. That's not just for the year after you win it either. It's forever. Not much is forever in this world.

Know what was impressive? The coaches and players started talking about winning another one in the locker room right after the game. I remember Bill saying, even though he retired after the game, "Okay, you guys won this one. Enjoy it for the next 24 hours or so, but then it's over and it's time to win another." That was always my mind-set, too, after winning that first one. With San Francisco and later Dallas, it was I won this, now it's done, I want to get ready for the next game. If we won a regular-season game on a Sunday afternoon, I'm watching film of the next opponent that night. As I've said, I was a very introverted person during my career, and for the most part, I went to work and I came home. There wasn't much partying or such. I might go grab a drink or two here and there, but that was about it.

After Coach Walsh retired, they hired my defensive coordinator, George Seifert, as the new head coach. Now, in retrospect, they could have brought in the ghost of Vince Lombardi or Moses, and I wasn't going to be thrilled. At the time I was a petulant child. Being bipolar certainly wasn't helping, but I was a long way from being diagnosed. I was a mess. I should have been the happiest man on the planet—and at times I was. Mostly though, I was miserable. Even on those rare days when I was smiling and telling jokes, I was dying inside.

There are a lot of stories about Coach Seifert and me involving the good, the bad, the more bad, the ugly, and the more ugly. I just want to say first that he's a good man, a kind soul, and he deserved better than the abundance of shitstorms he was forced to deal with because of me. People fear what they don't understand instead of trying to understand what they fear. And I was in constant fear. I didn't know what was going on with me.

We were more or less unstoppable in 1989. We finished 14–2 and could have easily won them all. We lost those two games by a combined five points. The talent on that roster was really unfair. Joe was at the top of his game, and when he came off the bench, Steve Young was pretty solid, too. Imagine having those two quarterbacks on the same team.

The first year wasn't that bumpy with George and me. We had known each other since I came into the league, though we didn't talk much. He knew I knew what I was doing, and Bill told his assistants not to bother me much. I certainly don't recall George ever saying anything negative toward me. Whatever he drew up, I did and I tried to do it to the best of my ability. He seemed good with that arrangement.

I have invented a lot of hate in my head over the years, and that was the case with Coach Seifert. I decided he must not like me because he didn't talk to me over the years. But I would have found a reason to dislike whoever the new head coach was.

I played pretty well that season—10.5 sacks, scored my lone career touchdown on a fumble recovery—and we rolled once again through the playoffs. We outscored our three postseason opponents by 100 points, including a massacre of the Denver Broncos in Super Bowl XXIV down in New Orleans. We won 55–10, and it wasn't even that close. That remains the largest margin of victory in Super Bowl history. So yeah, we beat the crap out of them. I honestly felt sorry for Denver's John Elway, who was a heck of a quarterback. He could extend a play as well as anyone I played against.

We had faced the Broncos the previous season and lost in overtime, but that helped me kind of understand what to expect with their offensive line. They were kind of well known for chop blocks, so once the game was out of control, I came out because I was tired of them trying to hurt me. I should also say that our offensive line did its share of cut blocking, too, so I'm not trying to call anyone out. It is what it is. For me cutting was the worst thing imaginable. Because I was so agile and mobile, I wasn't bull-rushing anyone. I jumped over and around a lot of chop blocks in my career and tried to out-quick them as best I could.

My specific memories from that Super Bowl are really just hitting John again and again and him throwing a couple of picks. The man didn't have a chance. We just kept hitting him. He was a tough dude. He stayed in there and took a punishing. Every time I turned around, we were scoring a touchdown. It was a three-and-out, touchdown, three-and-out, touchdown. If we kept our horses going, we could have scored 70. That's crazy to think about, but we were on another level that day.

I never did much celebrating after we won Super Bowls. Maybe I should have. I would just kind of sit at my locker and watch everyone with their champagne. I'd maybe drink a beer myself, take the scene in. I put so much pressure on myself to win that I was always more relieved than jubilant. My teams were supposed to win, so if we didn't, that meant I failed.

Honestly, I've never been a big drinker in general. I'm sure with all of those stories out there about me, people figured I was drunk half the time. I wasn't. When I drink, I'm very, very passive. I don't get angry about nothing. I just want to have fun. Everything in life is fun when I have a few drinks. Nothing brings me into rage-mode when I drink.

A big part of that, though, and I eventually realized this, was that the way I drank was probably different than anyone else you'll ever meet. I would drink a few beers real fast or do a couple of quick shots and then I would stop drinking. I was scared that one of my teammates or somebody else in the place was going to jump me because they thought I was drunk, so I went home. That's another example of how I lived in so much fear for most of my life. I just didn't understand at the time that my teammates had my back; they were my friends. There is no greater bond than teammates. I just didn't give anyone a chance to understand me—outside of Ronnie and a few others. I spent my career running away from those who were trying to just be my friend. That's sad to look back on.

Here's another example of where my mind was during those last few years with San Francisco. Each year, we would have a team bonding outing at Six Flags Great America in Santa Clara, which is where the 49ers headquarters was. And I happened to bump into Coach Seifert and his wife. And he introduced me to his wife by saying, "This is Charles. He never makes mistakes."

This really pissed me off.

How ridiculous is it to have that set me off? The man takes the time to introduce me to his wife, which few coaches ever have, and gives me a great compliment, and I was all sorts of furious. As I walked away, I took what he said as he was telling his wife that I was dumb. There was nothing positive in my mind from his words. I was thinking negative, negative, and more negative. I always thought that people figured athletes were dumb, especially me, so that's what I believed. It took me a while to figure out what people were really saying, long after my playing career was done, so I misinterpreted a lot of stuff. I also hated criticism, whether real or imagined.

Here's how much I hated criticism. Know how I mentioned earlier that I knew everybody's position and responsibilities on the field? Part of that was being able to help others, but to be honest, part of that was for me. If I knew what everyone was supposed to be doing on every play and I knew my job, then nobody could ever come and point the finger at me for making mistakes. I was motivated by the fear of criticism, which can actually be quite healthy. I, though, couldn't tell a younger version of Charles that. I was mobile, agile, and violent. And I used all of those weapons against everyone they put in front of me. Unfortunately, that went for foes and friends alike.

Speaking of my short list of friends—maybe mentor-friend is a better way of describing him—I really need to share my feelings about the then-owner of the San Francisco 49ers, Eddie DeBartolo Jr., who to my delight recently joined me as a member of the Pro Football Hall of Fame. I was ridiculously spoiled in terms of my two NFL owners, first Mr. D. and then Jerry Jones with the Cowboys. I assumed every owner was like them because I had nothing to compare them to, but players talk—be it at the Pro Bowl, the Super Bowl, charity events, whatnot— and there were some owners who didn't even know their players by name, let alone treat them like family members, sons really.

Mr. D treated us like the boys he never had—the best of us and the worst of us. That's important. I was a pretty damn good football player as were Joe, Jerry, and Ronnie, but Mr. D treated the punter the same way. The last guy on the practice squad was treated with the class the Pro Bowl guys were. That goes a long way. Mr. D was so consistent, too. He held that line every day. The man didn't have bad days. His idea of running a business was treating everyone like family. We were all in this together and not just the players. Ask his secretary, ask the public relations guy, the dude filling the vending machines at team headquarters. I promise you they all have a story about the kind of person Mr. D is.

A lot of teams in the 1980s were flying commercial and staying in mediocre hotels. Not us, not in the least. We practiced in the best facility in the league, top of the line. We rode the best buses and planes, stayed in five-star hotels, and all had single rooms. The food couldn't have been better. Mr. D never cut a corner with his team to save a buck. The man had our backs, and we would have walked through fire to have his. To this day, there is nothing he could call and ask me for that my immediate reply wouldn't be, "Yes, sir." I mean, he could say, "Charles, I need you to jump out of a plane naked and land in the middle of Siberia," and I'm stripping down before the phone call ends.

My first year in the league, even before my first game, Mr. D was great to me. He took me to Pebble Beach, he took me to Hawaii, he took me to Vegas. Hell, at that point, I hadn't been to shit or shine, so going anywhere was a big deal, but especially those places. He even tried teaching me to golf, but I was horrible. And everyone kept yelling at me for driving the cart onto the green. They said I couldn't drive on the green, but I said, hell, it's all green.

Mr. D took care of my family, and he also gave me Bill Walsh. He was the man who hired Bill, and Bill was my game changer. So there's a lot of love there, too. When Mr. D presented me at my Hall of Fame induction, he told this story, one I was actually going to tell. It happened late in the 1989 regular season against the Los Angeles Rams. The way he tells it, I was ejected from the game for unsportsmanlike conduct, and he came down to the locker room looking for me. And when he poked his head around the corner and said, "Charles," I looked up and said, "They ejected you, too, Mr. D?"

It's a funny story, but the real story is we were losing the game (we came back and won 30–27), and he put his foot through the Coca-Cola machine and then smashed the television. I saw that and was like, *Okay, I'm going to shower.* With my full uniform on. I just wanted out of there. I wasn't coming out until he was gone. Oh man, he's Italian, and they have some tempers. He was more pissed off than me, I can promise you that. For a guy like Mr. D, this rich and powerful owner and businessman, to take a nobody like me and put him under his wing, that says a lot. That says it all, really. I love him very much.

Of course, none of us knew it going in, but the 1990 season was the last hurrah for the nucleus of our dynasty. No one ever tells you the end is coming. It just kind of arrives. And you don't really have any control over it. We kicked our usual amount of ass during the regular season, again going 14–2 and ended up hosting a heck of a New York Giants team in the NFC Championship Game. Including the playoffs, we were 39–5 in our previous 44 games.

We had played one another earlier in the year, one of the highest-rated *Monday Night Football* games ever in fact. We won that one 7–3. Both defenses were playing so well that we were all expecting another low-scoring game. And that proved to be the case with seven field goals and just one touchdown accounting for the scoring.

The big play, though, didn't involve any points. It was a Roger Craig fumble with about three minutes left. We were leading 13–12 at the time and were at the Giants' 40-yard line. We were so close to playing for our third straight Super Bowl. No team to this day has won three straight. Instead, the ball just kind of popped out of Roger's grasp, and who else but Lawrence Taylor was right there to recover it. I think he caught it before the ball even hit the ground. He was so quick; his instincts and reaction time were unequalled.

The Giants picked up a few first downs and ended up kicking the winning field goal with no time left. We just couldn't stop them. No three-peat. Party over. I remember that game so well, maybe more than any of my career. As a competitor, you always remember the losses more than the wins.

I have always blamed myself for that loss. Everyone talks about Roger's fumble, but there was a play I should have made on that final drive. I was supposed to take the back—I think it was Dave Meggett, that little dude—and I rushed instead. He ended up catching the pass and picking up 10 yards. I just couldn't get to the quarterback in time. I made a judgment call, and it hurt us. That was the first time I really remember having a mental block during a game, making a poor decision. Now, off the field, there were multiple mental blocks every hour. On the field, though, football decisions were a sixth sense for me because of all the film and preparation.

Joe ended up hurting his back pretty badly in that game and he missed the entire 1991 season. I would never play with him again. And the team didn't re-sign Ronnie that offseason. He went to the Raiders, which really pissed me off. That's what led to me self-destructing. Honestly, at the end, I'm not entirely sure I didn't have a nervous breakdown. I was emotionally dead.

Losing Ronnie was a big part of it. That's when the anger really started boiling. I couldn't view it as a business decision. For me, that was personal. They let my best friend go, our team leader. Christ, the man had part of his pinkie amputated so he wouldn't miss any time in 1986, and four years later, it's "don't let the door hit your ass on the way to the Raiders." That just isn't right.

Look, I was a head case. We know that. And it would have been so much worse without Ronnie. I'm not sure what would have become of my NFL career if Ronnie hadn't been there when I arrived in San Francisco.

I like to break balls. That wasn't part of the bipolar disorder either, as I'm still doing it nowadays on my medication, though to a lesser degree. I didn't make fun of Ronnie, though, never. He was like a father, an older brother, and my own Yoda all in one. Friendships have always been so difficult for me. I was always second-guessing whether or not the guy was really a friend. I never did that with Ronnie, not for a second. No teammate ever influenced me more.

When Ronnie would mess with me, maybe in the film room or whatever, I would have to stand up and leave so I wouldn't go after him. Then he would come find me and slap me on the head and say, "You can do better than that, than just running away. We're friends. Stop being that way." And I would be okay. Anyone else, Volcano Charles would have erupted. Not with Ronnie.

As a player Ronnie was my example every day of what I wanted to be. Some guys are walking around the locker room, on the practice field, and you can see they are going through the motions sometimes. It's natural, really. Being a football player is just like any other job. There are certain days when you just can't crank it up to that 100 percent level. But Ronnie cared just as much every single day. He was just as intense watching film on a Monday as he was in the fourth quarter of the Super Bowl. On the first day of minicamp, Ronnie was strapping on that helmet like it was his last day to play football. I don't know how he possessed that kind of passion and drive 24/7/365, but he did. So I wanted to be like him. I tried my damnedest, too.

Know what else I took from Ronnie? And this is the greatest compliment you can say about an athlete: he played his best in the big games. Anyone can pick up a couple of sacks or big tackles against the Atlanta Falcons in September. Now where are you, come January? I want the January guys on my side. Ronnie is the best competitor and performer in big games that I ever played with, and I played with a lot of guys with busts currently residing in Canton.

I'm proud of my own record in big games, but that's for other folks to analyze.

I arrived at training camp in 1991 full of piss and more piss. I was angry at the world, even more than usual. And in my mind, it was all because of George Seifert. He sent Ronnie packing, he injured Joe's elbow, and now, he wanted me to step up and become a team leader. The nerve.

If I really look at the truth, Coach Seifert was trying to make me a better man. He wanted me to be a leader, which is what every great football player aspires to become, but everything that he wanted me to do, I didn't want to do. If I would have listened to him, I would have retired as a 49er. I would have been there until they couldn't drag me on the field any longer, but we just kept butting heads throughout the year. It was a mess. I was acting out more and more without Ronnie and Bill Walsh around. Those were the only two who could keep me under control.

I started really pushing my teammates—more so than ever before. In some ways, mostly on the field, I already was a leader. Off the field, I was the last person most of my teammates and coaches wanted to see. They think I was bad in Dallas a few years later? That was Gandhi on a hunger strike compared to me in 1991. A lot of guys, even football players, don't like to be hit in the mouth. You know the Mike Tyson line, right, about how everyone has a plan until they are hit in the mouth? Well, it makes a lot of sense. Hit a guy in the mouth, and more than anything, he becomes afraid. I wanted everyone afraid of me before they had a chance to piss me off.

And some of them, especially that season, I would even pop in their privates. Guess what happens then? When I open my mouth, everybody covers up and they look at me scared 14 different ways until Friday. Some people might say that's crazy, but you know what? You got to do what you got to do. It ain't about playing nice. It's about knocking Humpty Dumpty off the wall and tackling him. It's about winning the war, not that one battle but winning that war. And the only way you can do that is through knowledge. That team didn't have the knowledge we once did, and it showed on the field. We finished 10–6.

The nuclear explosion of all my meltdowns came in Week 5 when we were playing the Raiders and Ronnie in Los Angeles. We lost 12–6, which dropped us to 2–3. Hell, we hadn't lost three games the whole year in each of the last two regular seasons. This was unacceptable. I was angry the entire game, though after the game I hugged and kissed Ronnie on the field. My rage subsided just for that instance.

If you have never suffered a breakdown of any kind, consider yourself blessed. Let me attempt to explain it. All your hate, all your anger, all your anxiety, all your hopes, all your fears, all your dreams, and all your nightmares converge as one with the emotions boiling until you really lose mental consciousness. It was an out-of-body experience, and I wasn't in control.

I was so upset, so emotional that I was crying and shaking like never before. There was so much hate inside of me, and at that moment, it was coming out like never before. Teammates were trying to calm me down, and I was trying to hit them. Then Coach Seifert tried to grab my shoulder, and I was in such a rage, I kind of took a swing at him, too. I can't believe I did that.

I was swinging wildly at that point and I ended up putting my hand through a glass window with that wiring stuff inside, so I cut my arm and wrist up pretty badly. There was blood everywhere. The doctors and everybody were saying I needed medical help, but I wouldn't let anyone near me. I just sat there bleeding, feeling like whatever happened was meant to be. This was a full-fledged nervous breakdown.

Some of my teammates and a few of the doctors went to the Raiders locker room and found Ronnie. They knew he was the only one who could calm me down. It was so urgent that Ronnie had not even dressed. Well, Ronnie, who was still wearing a towel, came over, sat down next to me, and calmed me down enough to let the medical staff work on me. He actually held my hand while they were pulling the glass out and putting stiches in. I was still crying and shaking. Ronnie told me it was okay, that he appreciated how much I cared. As usual, he was the only one who understood me.

That was a tough episode for me. For the next few weeks, I was so emotional that I was crying all the time. My teammates started calling me "crybaby." At that point I'm sure the 49ers were thinking it was time for me to go, but I finished the season and was there at training camp in 1992.

Another problem for me that last year with San Francisco was our new starting quarterback, Steve Young. I was never a fan of his when we were teammates. I thought he was arrogant when he was traded to us from the Tampa Bay Buccaneers in 1987. He felt like we were his team when Joe was the captain of the team.

Steve just didn't mix with us, you know what I'm saying? He never tried to be a part of the team by laughing and joking or whatever. I don't like people like that, and maybe that's why we butted heads or whatever. We definitely didn't get along, not that I was really getting along with anyone my last season there.

I've seen Steve a few times since our playing days. I've seen him the last few years at the Super Bowl. And he was there when the 49ers presented me with my Hall of Fame ring, so we talked then. We're good now. I know I didn't play well with others back then. That's all in the past. We're done; we're old men now. What the hell, right? Everybody goes through things, and time heals all wounds. I think everything is good between Steve and me.

Here's the thing with me, especially back then. It was fight or flight, and I wasn't going to flee. I stood my ground. There wasn't anyone with that team, or in the NFL for that matter, who was going to do worse to me than my brothers had when I was growing up. Maybe everyone didn't realize that I was prepared for whatever happened. That was my state of mind.

I was also going to speak my mind. I didn't care if you were an All-Pro quarterback or the guy cleaning the jocks. I'd give both an equal amount of my wrath. I was also passionate, maybe more than I should have been, but you can't control passion.

I was, still am, passionate about making sure everybody, doesn't matter what side of the street you're from, realizes that they can achieve greatness if they choose to work hard. That's the part everyone has to buy into. You have to choose to work hard. You can't just show up and hope for the best. I chose to be around champions, around Joe, Ronnie, Bill Walsh, but the dynamics had changed so much by 1991. There were guys not willing to put the time in for us as a team to achieve greatness.

Coach Seifert was a micromanager. He would sit there and clean his glasses for 10 minutes before starting the film and then over the course of two hours explain what everyone should have been doing on each play. He knew all 11 assignments and who should have been where. That always impressed me.

He was the defensive coordinator when I arrived in San Francisco and he amazed me in the film room, so I wanted to be like him. That's where my motivation came to learn each position. My inspiration was his style of coaching. I tried to think like him, which was very detailed. And I did. I became immensely detailed about the mental aspect of not only my position, but also the entire defense. So looking back, we should have gotten along just fine. And we did for the most part over those first five years.

As for the official end with the 49ers, that came during the pre-season in 1992. There was a game in London, and I decided to just be difficult. I wasn't going. I told Coach I was staying home to have my knee scoped, but that was BS. That was kind of the last straw. You really can't tell a head coach what to do. This was less than a year after the meltdown following the Raiders game, too. I think Coach told the media it was best for team chemistry, which I understood.

I knew the trade was coming; they were just trying to get the best offer. Playing-wise, I was in my prime. It was just all the other stuff. I remember going to talk with Bill Walsh, who was then the head coach at nearby Stanford University, a few days before the trade was announced, and as always, I asked him what I should do. He wouldn't say.

It made me mad, but what he did say was pretty great stuff, especially looking back on it now. These words have always stayed with me.

He said, "If I tell you to stay and you're unhappy, you'll hate me. If I tell you to go and you don't have success, you are going to hate me. Charles, it's time for you to grow up, son. Make a decision and deal with it. Make the best out of however this works out."

The NFL Network did a beautiful documentary on my career in 2015, and Coach Seifert was nice enough to say that he made a mistake in trading me. He said he gave into his emotions at the time, that I had just become too disruptive to the team. He said he always liked me and that I was a great player for them. He also said he was sorry for having a weak moment. That was pretty powerful stuff for me. I definitely got a little teary-eyed hearing those words.

Let's be honest, though. As much as he's taking the high road, the reason I was leaving San Francisco was that I was an asshole.

George and I are okay now. We had a chance to talk when the 49ers were in the Super Bowl a few years ago in New Orleans. I told him that I was very sorry and about how much regret I have. We sat there for a while, and I just poured my heart out to the man. I wanted to make sure he knew I didn't hate him. I hated me back then. I wanted to make sure we both left this world knowing what really took place and that he knew it was on me. If I had listened to George, he would have shown me how to be a great leader.

Every time I see George now, the first words out of my mouth after we shake hands and hug are "I'm sorry." It doesn't matter how many times we see each other for the rest of our lives, those will always be my first words. And he's such a class act, he always tells me, "Yeah, you were tough, but I was a young coach and should have handled it better."

He's wrong. There's nothing he could do, and I tremendously regret how I treated him and my 49ers teammates that last year or so.

Chapter 6

Moving to Big D

BEING TRADED FROM the only pro team you have ever known sucks. Yes, I more or less forced the issue, but when it happens, when word comes down, it's like, damn, this is a whole new ballgame. I never envisioned myself playing for any other franchise besides the San Francisco 49ers. Even with my bitching and moaning, you can't visualize another reality until it becomes, well, a reality.

Then it happened. On August 26, 1992, I was traded to the Dallas Cowboys for draft picks. Yeah, draft picks. Less than 20 months earlier, I was named the NFC Defensive Player of the Year, and now here I was—the player to be named later.

At the time I was thrilled to just be out of San Francisco but was also scared beyond words. I knew nothing about Dallas. And I didn't follow the league like most guys. My focus was on my team and my family. I took a commercial flight to Dallas by myself, and when I walked into the terminal after landing, this man greeted me with a warm smile and heartfelt handshake. He claimed to be the owner of the Dallas Cowboys, but I had never heard of his name and figured he was full of it. The man could talk, though. If anyone could ever sell ice to Eskimos, it would be Jerry Jones.

He said he was there to drive me to the hotel I'd be staying at, which I later learned was located about three minutes from the gate at the airport. It took us like 90 minutes. First we were talking in his car, and then he was just aimlessly driving around the airport and then these side roads around the airport. I didn't know what was happening, but I enjoyed every minute of it. Jerry wanted to spend some quality time with me. I guess he wanted to see who the maniac was he traded for.

I came to Dallas humble because I didn't know what to expect. It didn't exactly end well in San Francisco, and you don't want to burn every bridge out there. But as I was getting into Jerry's car, I was think-ing, *Oh my God, this is incredible. The owner of a team came and picked me up at the airport. I must have hit the lottery again.* There is no doubt that I played for the two greatest owners in NFL history.

Jerry is something else, I'm telling you. There are a lot of misconcep-tions out there about the man. Yeah, he's the greatest salesperson I've ever been around, but he's kind, brilliant, funny, and patient, too. Jerry was, and is, like the grandfather I never had. He's that wise, old owl.

The thing that impressed me about Jerry more than anything was that he knew where he wanted to go. He told me the team was hemor-rhaging $100,000 a month when he bought it in 1989 and he couldn't just put a Band-Aid on it. He was telling me all this stuff on the ride from the airport. He explained the finances of the team, how the team was ready to win now, and that I was the last piece. He told me about how the famous Herschel Walker trade went down, about how head coach Jimmy Johnson did his homework on me and thought this was going to be a good situation.

Honestly, I think Jerry wanted to look me in the eyes and see what the hell he'd just done. To his credit, he immediately made me feel at ease by telling me point-blank, "You just play football, and I'll deal with any other problems myself. I have your back. We're going to be Super Bowl champions. Not down the road. We start today."

And that's what makes Jerry special as a businessman and as an owner. He takes chances. He always has. He was telling me on that same ride that when he was in the oil business, every hole they dug would cost him more than $100,000, so if that hole came up dry, that's some serious dough. He said the key was research, knowing which holes had the best chance of having some oil.

Jimmy and Jerry made their phone calls on me. They asked around to those who knew and played with me and felt like I was worth taking a chance on. I'm happy they did. My time in Dallas would be one of the greatest experiences of my life. I was told that Jerry called Mr. D and asked about me. Jimmy had his assistant coaches call the 49ers staff and then Jimmy even had his players call anyone they knew on San Francisco as well as guys who had moved on but played with me at one time. I guess they took three days making these calls, and the reports were basically the same: I was an intelligent player, I gave everything I had on the field, and I was completely bat-shit crazy. Jimmy and Jerry felt like that was doable.

In retrospect, there probably isn't a football coach in this world who, on paper, would be a worse fit for me. I did not like being yelled at. That's when I felt like someone was attacking me and I would go into attack mode myself as a result. And no one yelled more than Jimmy. He was an in-your-face screamer. At James Madison and with the 49ers, I was fortunate that the coaches realized this. I never heard Coaches Walsh or Seifert raise their voices. You could hear Jimmy from three blocks away.

Jimmy Johnson won a national championship at the University of Miami. His teams there were brash, in-your-face, and always quick. Jimmy loved quick players, especially on defense, so I was his kind of guy from that standpoint. While a master manipulator, a coach/psychologist really, Jimmy deserves credit for having the ability to treat his players differently. There wasn't a blanket set of rules. Well, there was, but if Michael Irvin or myself broke one of those rules, we were handled differently than some spare-ass benchwarmer.

However, that didn't mean Jimmy and I weren't going to butt heads. For the most part, though, he let me be me, and I love him for that. I was a mess back then, and he understood. The first season was tough, too, because Karen and my two kids stayed in California until the offseason, so I was alone in a new city. Jimmy is an alpha dog, and obviously, I was an alpha dog. So you know what? We had to see who was No. 1.

Also, we both thought one of the keys to success was keeping everyone uncomfortable. He had his methods, and I had mine. We had a few face-to-face combat screaming confrontations, but for the most part, we did all right. That man could talk. He probably said three times as many words per minute than any coach I have ever met.

My issue with Jimmy had to do more with his staff. The defensive coaches, they were weak. They would run back to Jimmy instead of talking with me. Then Jimmy would come tell me what they said. Does that make any sense? I still don't understand that. They wouldn't just call me back to their offices. Then one of them, or Jimmy, would call me out in front of the entire team at practice or while watching film.

I didn't understand that either because you're not going to talk to me or communicate with me in front of people. I'm shutting down, especially back then. If you want to close the doors, so we can have a discussion, I'm good with that. When I give you 100 percent every game, you're not going to talk to me with disrespect. And that's the secret to life. I'm pretty sure on multiple occasions I advised several of those assistant coaches to fuck right off. I don't need that crap. I'm guessing that's how Jimmy told them to deal with me, though. Jimmy ran that place like a dictatorship, so they were probably just following his orders.

The defense in Dallas was more simplistic than Coach Seifert's—even with the position change for me from outside linebacker to defensive end. Honestly, they are more or less the same; it just depends on whether it's a 3-4 or 4-3 scheme, meaning how many down linemen you have. I didn't have a preference. I honestly didn't care because I could do both. George Seifert wanted me to go down, put my hand on the ground, and so I did. With the 49ers, I could line up anywhere. They invented a position for me, so I was always moving around. John Madden used to keep track of where I was lined up when he did my games, which I always took as a great compliment. He was always nice to me for whatever reason. He's a good man.

With Dallas, it was more about just playing defensive end on the right side and standing up. Again, that never was a problem. Out of all my issues with coaches over the years, and there were plenty, none of them involved the X's and O's of football. Find me a single coach who says I didn't run the play exactly the way they wanted, that I argued about where they put me. That was the easy part. Charles the football player was quite coachable really. Charles off the football field was another story.

Football is fun. The practices, the games, the film, I loved it all. It was so much fun that I get goose bumps to this day just thinking about walking on the field. I loved it all—the pain, the agony, the success. I loved the turmoil, I loved the fighting, I loved busting balls. Without all that, I'm not sure there would have been many enjoyable days for me. Football has always been my drug of choice. I love the game so much.

My favorite memories aren't the Super Bowl wins either. Looking back, the best thing for me was playing on real grass, and your uniform was full of dirt and mud at the end of the game. That was exhilarating. It was like nothing else in this world was taking place except that football game. And you were going to give everything your body and mind would allow. I would always tease the other defensive linemen after the games about who had the most grass stains on the backs of their jerseys. That meant they were taken down the most by the offensive linemen. We called those pancakes. Russell Maryland even had a little song verse he would sing, "we are going down, down, down." We had a lot of fun, we really did.

That first season with the Cowboys, I was the first one there and the last one to leave. I watched film for hours upon hours. In the beginning I figured I needed to because it was a new defense, but that took me only a week or so. We ran like four plays. So then I decided to make sure I knew what the other 10 guys were doing on each of those plays. A lot of guys, they watch film, but they don't know what the hell they are looking at. It's like church—many attend; few understand. There are so many little things taking place from the sets and packages to when a blocker has a tendency to rise up, which allows you to explode under him using leverage.

Here's the deal: this wasn't James Madison, where I was the best athlete on the field. Everyone is big and fast in the NFL, so you have to find the opponent's weakness, and when you do, keep sticking it to him. Then, if he tries to protect that weakness, he creates another weakness. Perhaps more than anything else with the Cowboys, I tried to teach the other defensive linemen about watching film. Leon Lett would watch film with me for hours and he became a Pro Bowl guy who is now an assistant coach with the Cowboys. Tony Tolbert, Russell Maryland, Chad Hennings, Jimmie Jones, Tony Casillas, we all would watch film as much as any position group on the team.

I ain't going to say I was loved or anything. I might not have even been liked, I don't know. But what I do know is it was about winning. We finished with the top-ranked defense in the NFL during that 1992 season, allowing the fewest yards in the league, and that defensive line was a big reason why. And guess how many of our guys were named to the Pro Bowl? How about zero. What a joke. I'm not just talking about the defensive line either. Like no one from the defense was named at all. No worries. That just pissed us off more.

We were a tight group, the defense that is. What you need to understand is there are three divisions in an NFL locker room: offense, defense, and special teams. On the defensive side of the room, we rule each other. The offense rules themselves, and special teams is doing their thing. It's no one guy having the pulse of the entire team. Troy Aikman and Michael Irvin were the leaders of the offense, and I certainly tried to handle the defense in terms of watching film and teaching guys what it took to win a Super Bowl. I was the only guy in that locker room with a ring.

I'm not a big speech kind of guy, though. If somebody has to give you a damn speech to get you to go out and play, then you really don't love the game. When they gave them rah-rah speeches, I went to the nearest corner and sat my ass down. I didn't want to be a part of that crap. I knew what I was going do. I knew what I was leaving on the field for my team and the fans. A lot of these guys need that false courage. What am I going to say? Hey guys, rah, rah, ree, let's go take a piss. *That's going to win us a football game? Come on, are you for real?* That just wasn't me. And again, not to sound like a broken record, but I didn't play well with others.

Know what else doesn't make sense to me? So we go out to practice and try to break each other's damn neck all week, and then on Sunday, I'm supposed to say, 'oh, I love you, please be my Valentine?' Screw that. My family was the defense, and I needed to be focused entirely on them. I needed to know what everyone was supposed to be doing on each play, so I could help with any questions. I didn't have time to be sitting around talking trash with some fourth-string running back. Now, if people talked trash about me or to me, they very quickly wished they hadn't. I believe in leading by example. I'm not a man of words. I'm a man of action.

There were many weeks when our toughest competition came during our Thursday and Friday practices, the pad days. Jimmy ran those as if they were games, and if he didn't like something, he'd start the whole damn practice over. I remember multiple instances when we're an hour into practice, and someone made a mental mistake—he hated mental mistakes—and that man restarted practice. We would sit around in a circle and go stretching again. I'm thinking this guy is nuts. He set standards in those practices like nothing I have ever experienced. We were just out there beating the piss out of each other.

My body took more of a pounding during Jimmy's practices than on Sundays during those first two years in Dallas. I can't believe we didn't have more injuries. I like the Bill Walsh approach of no pads. We only wore pads in San Francisco for pass-rushing drills, which was once a week at most. The Friday before Super Bowl XXVII, Jimmy ran the toughest practice I've ever seen. The Buffalo Bills were likely going through a walk-through, and we're tackling each other like in *Any Given Sunday* or *The Longest Yard*.

There was never, ever an easy late-week practice with Jimmy. Through the Collective Bargaining Agreement, the league doesn't allow that anymore. They have restrictions on the number of practices with pads. I'm not sure how Jimmy would coach nowadays, but I assure you he would be successful. He would find another way to win.

We went 13–3 that first season and should have gone 15–1. We were only outplayed once that entire year, and that was at the hands of the Philadelphia Eagles in Week 5. We adopted, maybe inherited, the attitude of our head coach. We were cocky, some would say obnoxious, but guess what? We backed it up. We kicked some serious ass on Sundays.

I've played on some talented football teams. We twice won 14 games in San Francisco, but that first Dallas team, I've never seen that much talent in my life. It was something else, a sight to behold. I'm not a football historian, but I'd put that team up against anyone. I don't do much bragging. It's not my thing, but when people start talking about this team or that team being the best or whatever, I just smile.

Our offense scored the second most points in the league. You could honestly make the case that we had the best offense and best defense in the NFL. That's ridiculous. How does that happen? Jimmy and Jerry, that was a dangerous combination before they started fighting and bickering like those two dudes on the balcony from *The Muppets*.

We had Emmitt Smith as our running back, who to this day is the league's all-time leading rusher. That record isn't being broken either. Troy Aikman was our quarterback, and always jaw-jacking Michael Irvin was our big-dog wide receiver. Daryl "Moose" Johnston was a heck of a fullback, and Jay Novacek was a Pro Bowler at tight end. That team was so loaded it was almost unfair.

The offensive line, led by my buddy Nate Newton, might have been the best offensive line during my time in the league, and it made us better going against them every day. Hell, gameday was easy. Nate usually had two guys coming at him and would still block them both. He never was fully appreciated, and the center, Mark Stepnoski, who was like six feet and 250 pounds, was a master technician. Then there was tackle Erik Williams, the "Big E," and that monster punch. He dominated Reggie White like no other man.

I like Troy. I always have. I'm not sure he liked me at first, though I could always make him laugh. When I first arrived in Dallas, I would mess around with him at practices and in the locker room, saying, "You're no Joe Montana, that's for sure." Crap like that. It came out as this big national media story, and I'm like, please, that's just me being me. It's not like I went up to his locker and started a fight. He would throw a nice ball in practice, and I'd say it joking around, but also to try to push him. I like to push people. I want to see if you have fight in you. I think I might have hit him hard in practice once because I was angry about a few interceptions he threw the previous week. Maybe that's when the story came out that I was treating Troy poorly and whatnot. That's simply not true.

Before our games, I would talk, talk, talk, and talk some more. I was trying to burn some of that energy I was feeling and also take some stress off people who were nervous. Nothing relieves stress better than laughter. For me, the happier I am, the better mind-set I have. That's why I watch cartoons. They make me laugh, and then I forget about what I'm about ready to do until it's actually time to do it. That's what I was trying to accomplish, reverting back to my class clown days in school.

We had this one team doctor, and he had a rather large head. Honestly, it might have been the biggest head I've ever seen. It was Halloween of 1993, and we were playing the Eagles that day. I was calling him the Great Pumpkin. I said, "We'll cut your head open and put a lantern in there, and you'll be the real-life Great Pumpkin." Troy was standing there next to me, and he was laughing so hard he swallowed his snuff, which was in his lower lip. He ran to the bathroom, still laughing, and then threw up.

I was always telling guys I was the Wizard of Oz and that they needed to follow the yellow brick road. I'd be walking around calling guys the Scarecrow or the Lion because some were looking for brains and others needed courage. There were a lot of guys dumber than a box of rocks. We had linebackers saying they were making the defensive calls, which was crap because they hardly knew their playbook. We made it all work, though. I pushed them. I pushed every button I could think of.

What was difficult, though, was that I didn't really hang out with the guys away from football. So they would be telling stories from this party or that, and I couldn't really join in the conversation. I was having too many kids, and Karen made sure I came home after practice after she and the kids moved from San Francisco following that first season. Really, the most I ever did was go to a local restaurant, the Cowboys Sports Café, and eat, maybe have a few beers.

If there was someone I hung out with, it might have been Nate. We were always telling jokes and ripping on each other. I called him the "Big Vending Machine." I would kick him in the ass, and peanuts, Cokes, and fried chicken would fall out. A Snickers bar once fell out of his pants during a game. He was hilarious. My running joke with Nate was that we were going to dig a pit, put a rod up his ass, and then roast him like a hog. Nate and left tackle Mark Tuinei were really good guys to talk to and hang out with. Tuinei was the "Dancing Bear." He'd do what looked like a dance when I would put a move on him in practice. I kept telling him he was wasting his time dancing with me. I was already married.

Michael and Emmitt were more high-profile guys. They lived in their own world for the most part, but we got along. Michael always would hang out with the guys, and that was good or bad. (There are some stories from the bad.) Emmitt, on the other hand, you would see him every blue moon. Michael and I were cool. Michael was cool with everyone. He was probably hanging out with the kicker and punter, and I didn't even know their names. Michael was the ultimate teammate. He was a part of all of us. He drank with us; he broke bread with us. He was an entertainer, the "Playmaker." I spent some fun nights with him before Karen and the kids moved to Dallas after that first season.

I used to ride Emmitt and tell him he wasn't Barry Sanders. I'd tell him in front of the entire team, "Barry Sanders is the greatest running back in this era." I had to find out where guys were mentally, so I challenged them. Make no mistake, though, Emmitt is a tough son of a gun. He showed everyone how great he was, often in the biggest games. He played that one game against the New York Giants with a separated shoulder. I've never seen another running back do that.

I never really got to know Emmitt during our playing days, but our kids played soccer and stuff together, and now we talk all the time. I realize now that he always wanted to be my friend, but I wouldn't let him. I did that to a lot of people. I attacked before I could be attacked. The sad part is 99 percent of the time nobody was even thinking about attacking me, but I was always on edge, always afraid.

I love my teammates. I always thought people took your kindness for weakness, so I never tried to let people know that side of me because I didn't want them to take advantage of it. It was one of my many mistakes during my playing career because those were some of the best people you could ever be friends with.

So after winning our first playoff game in 1992 with ease, guess who our opponent was in the NFC Championship Game? Yep, the San Francisco 49ers, who finished 14–2 in the regular season, meaning we were headed to Candlestick Park, my old home field. But this time I was the enemy. To say I entered that game wanting revenge, wanting to prove my worth, is probably obvious. In my mind Coach Seifert thought he could put anybody in my position on that defense and they could replicate my performance, my impact on a game.

There was definitely a sense of vindication for me after we beat them 30–20. The game was a thriller, one of the most memorable of my career, and it came down to the end. We were up by less than a touchdown in the fourth quarter with fewer than four minutes to play when Troy hit Alvin Harper on a 70-yard bomb and then three plays later found Kelvin Martin in the end zone to seal the win. Troy was magnificent. I hope I told him that after the game, but knowing me, I probably didn't.

The 49ers tried every dirty trick possible to hurt me. They chop blocked me, they hit me from behind, they hit me after the whistle. They were trying stuff that I had never seen. They were obsessed with stopping me. My teammate, Tony Casillas, had three sacks because they were sending the guard and tackle to block me, letting our defensive tackles run free. I hit Steve Young a couple of times, and then he started running up into the line, trying to escape. He ended up throwing two interceptions, which made a big difference.

I wanted that win as much as any game I ever took the field for. I was so emotional that I cried after. I just wanted to make sure the 49ers really understood how much I meant to that team and that they made a mistake trading me. I couldn't be replaced with some rookie off the street or some joker like that. I really wanted to put a stamp on it. I wanted them to know that they could gameplan for me all week—and they did—that they could do whatever the hell they want, but they couldn't stop me.

★ ★ ★

A Super Bowl always felt like a regular-season game for me. However, a singer is most definitely not just another singer. Especially when his name is Michael Jackson. And he was playing at the Super Bowl in the

Rose Bowl on January 31, 1993, and I wasn't going to miss that show. Luckily, it was taking place at halftime of Super Bowl XXVII. That was unbelievable. I'm back in the Super Bowl with my new team. We just beat my old team to get there, and, oh yeah, Michael Jackson is playing. When I was growing up in Gladys, there were in terms of faraway possibilities—graduating college, flying to the moon, and meeting Michael Jackson. For me, each of those was as unrealistic as the next.

The reason I wore one glove during the majority of my playing career was in honor of Michael because I wanted to be a thriller like him. So I wasn't missing him at halftime. Leon, Michael Irvin, and a few of us came out of the tunnel to watch him perform. It was just ridiculous. He moved nations with his music, and I've been a big fan since the Jackson 5 days. I was just blessed to be there to watch him in action once again. The 49ers played a preseason game in London in 1988, and he was there the same week on the *Bad* tour. I was able to go down under the stage afterward and meet him, take a few pictures. They told me we had to stay a certain number of feet away and all this crap. He had these two ginormous Samoans as his bodyguards; these guys made me look like Gary Coleman. Those were the two biggest brothers I have ever seen to this day. And I said, "I don't care what you all do to me, I'm meeting Michael." I walked over and hugged him and brought Karen up, and we took photos.

After we were introduced by one of his people, Michael says in this really, really soft voice that his brothers like football. I couldn't believe that he could speak that soft with that powerful singing voice. I was shocked. And I mean, he looked like he weighed 60 pounds, God bless him. He was a twig, but he was tall and had big hands. I was like, wow, I was impressed like never before. I wouldn't have cared if he had a turd on the top of his head, I would have still been impressed. He had me and he always did. He was my idol.

That week in Los Angeles for the Super Bowl was a mess. Yeah, a lot of guys got in trouble, oversleeping, missing meetings, and missing in general. I kept my routine the same. For all the big, bad Charles talk over the years, anyone ever remember me being in trouble? I've never been arrested, never in trouble with the league, never suspended, none of that stuff.

So that week, I didn't deal with the media. Yes, shocking I know, but screw them. I spent my free time with my family. My wife, the kids, my parents, and brothers came out. I didn't have any friends coming, so that made it even easier. I was there to do a job and win a football game. And see Michael sing. The first few days were chaos, the stories were legendary, but I was in bed early. I kept it simple. During the craziness of the first few days, the guys just didn't know how to handle the bedlam of a Super Bowl week, and being in L.A. didn't help. The last few days, though, we moved from the hotel where our families were into a separate place, and that's when Jimmy put his foot down on guys' necks and we refocused on the game.

I almost forgot about our opponent, the Buffalo Bills. They were nice guys, some great players, but in terms of having a chance to beat us, we had already played our Super Bowl two weeks earlier. The Bills were like a high school team compared to the 49ers.

Our confidence level went out the roof—or through the roof. Wherever the hell it goes with the roof, we were there and then some. No one was beating us that afternoon. We were all Superman. Those bullets can't kill you, and you're invincible. I've played a lot of football games, and only once did I feel invincible. That was it. And I bet you a lot of my teammates felt the same.

When I arrived in Dallas, my first day there, a few of my new teammates asked me to bring in one of my Super Bowl rings, so they could see it. I said, "You morons, win one. Win your own." I was a jerk even by my standards about that. But seeing someone else's ring just divides the team. It's not bringing us together. My thing was *we* need to win one.

I don't want to hear about you wanting to see what I've got. Hey, let's win our own, and man, God knows we possessed the ability to do so.

We had the talent, the speed, the mind-set. I don't doubt we could have won four straight. Jimmy's ass should be in the Hall of Fame because he took the youngest team in the league to the house. They changed the rules with free agency and the salary cap to stop Jimmy and Jerry from league domination. That's all because of how great that 1992 team was. When they change the rules, you know you're doing something right.

When people ask me about Super Bowl XXVII, I end up telling stories about the week before the game and Michael, but there was a game, and we kicked ass 52–17. We should have broken the record for largest margin of victory that my 49ers set a few years earlier, but my good friend Leon had some issues en route to the end zone, and Don Beebe caught up to him and forced a fumble. Poor Leon, he's one of the better defensive linemen of his generation, and that's the clip you always see.

The Bills actually led 7–0, and then we tied it up. With a minute or so left in the first quarter, Buffalo's quarterback, Jim Kelly, dropped back toward his end zone to pass, and I leveled him from the blind side. Jimmie Jones caught the ball and ran it in for the score. The rout was soon on.

In the locker room after we beat Buffalo, a reporter asked me something about how much I was going to enjoy the offseason after having won my third Super Bowl. I should have gone with my usual response of, "Screw off," but I didn't. Instead, I responded, "First off, the game's over, so that's in the past. It's time to start focusing on next season and going back-to-back. Anything less than another championship would be deemed a disappointment, and I don't plan on having any disappointment in my life."

There is nothing more difficult in sports than winning consecutive titles because everyone is coming for you. Everyone is giving you his best. That 3–8 team? Well, their Super Bowl is playing you. There are no off days, no easy games. That first season in Dallas was kind of like a honeymoon for me, for the entire team, really. The second, not so much. And there was a divorce on the horizon that never, ever, ever should have taken place.

Chapter 7

Going Back-to-Back with the 'Boys

SAN FRANCISCO IS a beautiful city, and the fans there couldn't have been nicer to my family and me. Heck, Karen and the kids didn't want to move when I was traded; it took them almost a year to join me. The people are chill, relaxed, and knowledgeable. I don't have a negative thing in the world to say about San Fran.

It's just that, and this isn't a bad thing, the day-to-day trials and tribulations of the 49ers aren't the biggest things in anyone's lives out there—except for maybe the players and coaches. The fans want the 49ers to win, but on Monday, it's back to their world, their jobs, their families.

In Dallas, and really Texas in general, the Cowboys are the lead story 365 days a year. I have never seen anything like it. There was no place I could go during my playing days there without being recognized and asked for an autograph. I mean, homeless dudes were asking me and I'd say, "How about $10 instead?" and they were like, "Nah, I'll take the autograph."

My old college assistant coach, the man who recruited me and changed my world, Danny Wilmer, came to visit me in Dallas. I think he was coming to the game, and so we went out for dinner Friday night. I told him that it wasn't a good idea, that we should order takeout, but he wanted some authentic Tex-Mex, so off we went.

We were there five minutes, hadn't even gotten the chips and salsa yet, and I'm signing for 80-year-old women, kids who were still pooping their diapers, and everyone in between. We left after an hour without eating. It was just bedlam. And I was a freaking defensive end. Imagine what Troy Aikman, Emmitt Smith, or Michael Irvin went through.

Someone told me that first year that the three most popular sports in Texas in order are high school football, college football, and the

Dallas Cowboys. That sounds about right. They are obsessed with their football. And in 1993, for like two months, the lead story on every television, radio, and newspaper was Emmitt's contract holdout. Presidential elections don't receive the kind of coverage this did. It was mind-boggling. It only intensified after we lost our first two games, the latter of which came against the Buffalo Bills in a rematch of the previous Super Bowl. What happens next depends on who you ask.

The version that went viral, at least what was considered viral back then before the Internet, was that I threw my helmet at Jerry Jones as I walked into the locker room and said, "We're trying to defend the world championship with a rookie running back and one of the greatest ever is sitting at home watching on TV."

My helmet, and this part is true, made quite a hole in the wall, which was visible to the media when they were allowed in a few minutes later. That story was nice and neat, makes for good copy—Haley loses his mind again. The way I remember it, though, is that the offensive line was whining about how we couldn't win because Emmitt wasn't here and all this making excuses and crap, so I got up in front of them and started yelling. I said, "If Emmitt was hurt, we would have to pick him up. You all are whining like we can't win a football game without this one guy. We have to win with who we have." I was mad as hell—and at that moment—I lost my cool and threw the helmet.

I guess, and I was told this afterward, that Jerry was in the general direction of my toss, like two feet from where the helmet hit the wall. Everyone then wants to act like I was throwing the damn helmet at Jerry. I just threw the helmet because I wanted them to understand that it doesn't matter who is here. We can win.

But the media was given the story, and it was "Charles threw a helmet at Jerry." Man, that pisses me off to this day. Jerry's been good to me. He's been so absolutely good to me. When he picked me up at the airport, he said, "I got your back." The owner of the Dallas Cowboys said that. The only other man who told me that was Bill Walsh, you know what I'm saying? And that turned out okay, so I didn't have anything to worry about it. I adore Jerry and he knows that.

Know what else? No one wants to win more than Jerry. He likes to make a buck, but trust me, he likes to win even more. And three days later, he signed Emmitt. We went 15–2 the rest of the season, including the playoffs. That year was definitely different than the first Super Bowl run. First off, the pressure was ridiculous; everyone expected perfection. We weren't supposed to lose a game once Emmitt came back.

But even when the Cowboys aren't great, every team gets up to play them. That star on the helmet, on the field, on the uniform brings more pressure than any other job in sports because you are representing America's Team, not just Dallas or Texas. And that rang true. You should have seen us on road games. Holy God, half the crowd was cheering for us, fans attacked the buses. We were rock stars. We were the Jackson 5 and the Beatles rolled into one. It took me time to fully appreciate what that star represented. It took me time to understand the size of the fanbase, and how what we did on the field meant so much to so many. It's an incredibly humbling and proud honor. We always got the other team's A game. I would watch film of the team from the week before—this happened all the time—and I'd be like, we're going to kill them; this team sucks. But we'd barely end up beating them because you forget sometimes that those guys have pride just like you do, and if they're going to play one great game in their entire careers, it's going to be against the Dallas Cowboys. We were always on national television, too.

Now that we've straightened out the helmet toss with Jerry thing, know that the biggest disagreement Jimmy Johnson and I ever had was in December 1993. We were playing the Minnesota Vikings up there, and my back was really hurting. I told the coaches I would only play if they absolutely needed me to, which I guess was leaving the door open when I should have just shut it down for the week.

I was on the active roster, so I was eligible to play, but when the game started, I was on the sideline with just my leg pads and jersey on. No shoulder pads, no helmet. After the first quarter, we're losing 6–3, and Troy, Emmitt, all those guys are talking to me about how the defense isn't the defense without me, about how I have to play because we're battling the New York Giants to win the NFC East title, and we want home-field advantage in the playoffs. I warmed up a little, and it felt doable, meaning I could stand up and walk, so I put some pads on and went out there. I kicked some ass, too, made some plays, even had a sack, and we won, 37–20.

The Vikings head coach at the time was Denny Green, who was an assistant with the 49ers when I was there, and he brought a lot of guys over from San Francisco for his staff in Minnesota. I went over after the game and talked with a few of them, shook hands, etc. After a few minutes, I walk back to the locker room and I'm walking kind of slow with my back. I couldn't even jog at that point. I was like an old man once the adrenalin of the game wore off and was in a lot of pain. So I walk in, and Jimmy is in there screaming. You would have thought we lost by 30 points. We couldn't win by enough points to keep him happy.

In the middle of him yelling, he sees me walk in and says, "Get your ass over here." So I turned around and walked back toward the door, trying to see who the hell he was talking to. I didn't see anybody, so I figured whoever he was talking to must have run away. Just to make sure, though, I opened the door and looked in both directions. Still no one. As I turned around, Jimmy yells even louder, "I told you to get your ass over here!"

Jimmy was standing on this little raised stage or platform. I walked over and jumped up and got right in his face, I mean like an inch or two away. And I said, "Is this fucking close enough?" Everyone jumped in and separated us. We didn't talk for a few days.

When I look back, I should have never done that because Jimmy is a great guy, and we all know he was one hell of a great coach. I just didn't do well with confrontation. Jimmy was always telling me I was one of his guys, that he would always be there for me, and he was. I just don't understand the confrontation or the need to do it after a big win.

I've heard Jimmy talk about this since, that he couldn't help himself. That's the only way he knew how to coach, and maybe he thought we were becoming cocky after winning that first Super Bowl. I just figured maybe he could chill out a little. I don't know about the three years before I arrived, but Jimmy yelled and screamed more during that 1993 season than every other coach I had in my entire life combined.

★ ★ ★

Everyone loves statistics, but for defensive players, they are so misleading. I only had 10 sacks over those first two years in Dallas. I tallied more than that in six other individual seasons of my career. Know what, though? I never played at a higher level than those first two years. I was seeing double-teams on almost every play. Offenses were game-planning for me. Their plan was to stop Charles and take their chances elsewhere. Guys were always trying to hurt me, get me off the field.

I tell guys all the time, "Don't ball your fists up until the game starts and then don't un-ball them until it's over." That's the way I played. I didn't have time to be celebrating on the field or any of that crap. I was there to do my job, win the game, and go home. If we were winning by a few touchdowns, no one was coming off the field quicker than me. I could have stayed out there and padded my stats like a lot of guys do, but the physical pounding I was dealing with week to week was really starting to take a toll on my body. I owed it to the fans, to Jerry Jones, my teammates, and my coaches to stay healthy enough to be there when it mattered. That's where my commitment was, not toward picking up a few extra sacks.

Our defense ended up allowing the second fewest points in the league, and we won our last five regular-season games before knocking off Green Bay and San Francisco in the playoffs. The 49ers must have been scratching their heads by then. *Let's see, what changed from when we were winning Super Bowls? Oh yeah, Charles left. And who started winning Super Bowls? The team Charles went to.* That was certainly something I was proud of.

We played Buffalo in the Super Bowl again, and man, that was a much tougher game. I think they had a really superb gameplan for us. I think having beaten us earlier in the year helped them. I love Emmitt, but James Washington was the MVP of Super Bowl XXVIII. His fumble recovery in the third quarter after Leon Lett knocked the ball loose changed the entire game. They were driving around midfield and were already beating us by a touchdown. If they had scored there, even a field goal, it likely would've become one of those last-possession-type of games.

Buffalo really came in with a solid plan for keeping me in check. They double-teamed me on passing downs. Even on running plays, the tight ends chipped me. More or less, they were going to force someone else up front to make plays. Even with all that attention, I still had half a sack and a few tackles. I was pretty nervous about that game until the fourth quarter. The Bills came to play that day, and it was hard fought on both sides. I honestly think both teams showed up to win. That wasn't the case the year before. That was the fourth straight Super Bowl for Buffalo, too, and I don't care that they didn't win any of them; that's still a heck of an accomplishment.

I took a few cracks that game. That season, really. I turned 30 a few weeks before that Super Bowl, and let me tell you, the body of a 30-year-old pass rusher in the NFL isn't exactly like a 30-year-old accountant or salesman. I was hurting. I could barely practice during the week. I was more just watching film and doing some coaching of the younger guys. My body was breaking down big time, especially my back and my knees.

As my playing years went by, I never worried about the first guy, my initial blocker that is. It was the second guy. I could, in my mind, beat that first guy, but then the worry was about beating the second guy because that's when they would hit you right at your hip and pop that hip out. That's how I initially, and many times again, popped my back.

They didn't hit you up in the shoulders. I used to be a knee-bender, but after my first back surgery, I couldn't bend like I used to. So then I had to find new ways to rush the passer. I had to become more innovative. That's where all that film study of other pass rushers became so useful to me. There were some games by that second year in Dallas when I would try 15 different techniques, whereas in my early years, there were two or three I would use the entire game. I had to reinvent myself based on what I could still do physically.

My first step was still pretty good, and then each year going forward, I tried to find ways to adapt, to improve as the season progressed. I definitely worked on my first step more than anything else because that's the key to success. That first step dictates winning or losing.

And the key to that first step is timing the snap. Before the game even starts, I already knew their tendencies, I knew their backfield sets, I knew nine times out of 10 what was coming at me. Knowledge was everything.

Secondly, when I lined up, I never, ever looked directly at the ball. I saw the ball out of the corner of my eye in my peripheral vision. I saw the offensive tackle, quarterback, and running back, too, and then if there was motion, I saw that coming, whether it was a tight end or receiver. When the motion stops, the ball is going to be snapped on the next signal, so I could anticipate that and jump off. If there's no motion, you try and watch the quarterback's eyes, or when the running back starts his break. I tried to use everything to my advantage.

I would tilt in my stance where it would look like I was going to go inside, so the tackle had to make a decision to either jump out and take me or protect the inside. Whatever he did, I made sure it was wrong, even if it was a run. If he attacked me, I would jump inside, bend right back down the line of scrimmage, and catch the back before he got up-field. I had a ton of tackles for loss.

While some pass rushers just rushed the passer, I was pretty solid against the run. Some guys would finish with 20 tackles for the entire season, 15 of which were sacks. But I averaged more than five tackles a game during my first 10 years in the league. Offenses were wasting their time running at me, that's for sure.

The offensive tackle always moves before the ball. Look for that the next time you are watching a game. The tackle hears the call and starts moving before the center can start the act of moving the football, so I always keyed on the tackle. Well, that's not true. In college and when I came into the league, I used the ball as my key, but I learned because of the chop, the blocks, and the stuff that was coming at me to key on the tackle, so I would have more in my vision. That really helped me a lot. I think I made that change in my second year.

★ ★ ★

As everyone already knows, less than two months after winning our second straight Super Bowl, Jerry and Jimmy decided they couldn't coexist any longer. Despite having assembled possibly the most talented football team the world has ever seen, Jimmy was either fired or he quit, depending on who is telling the story. It doesn't really matter how it went down. They screwed us. It was like two women on one of those bad soap operas arguing about who stands where in a picture. Or two little kids bickering about who gets the bigger ice cream cone. Who gives a crap? Everyone is getting ice cream, be happy.

We could have won four straight Super Bowls with Jimmy. There's no doubt in anyone's mind who was on that team. Now, I don't think I would have been there for all of them. I think Jimmy probably would have cut me or traded me. I don't think he wanted to deal with me much longer.

Jerry hired the same guy who coached his and Jimmy's freshman team at Arkansas back in the day, Barry Switzer. And let me tell you, he was the greatest. He took a lot of bull from the fans and media, but he came in and did what Jerry wanted. And he treated us like men, which we appreciated. Well, for a lot of guys, though, he wasn't Jimmy. He couldn't have been more different. Barry was a players' coach. I'm guessing much more so than when he was at Oklahoma and was winning all of those national titles. He was pretty relaxed, except on gamedays. He could work the officials just like Jimmy and with more colorful language.

Some guys were used to having their necks stepped on by Jimmy at every turn. The yelling and screaming, you become accustomed to that, so for the guys who had been there three or four years, it took them some time to understand this new style. Barry was there to keep us running, let the coordinators and assistant coaches run the units, and just kind of oversee it all.

That's the same kind of situation that George Seifert stepped into when they let Bill walk. He came in the year after we won a Super Bowl in San Francisco. That's a tough gig, but at least George had been there, knew the players, the staff, the situation. Barry knew nothing. He was home on his couch in his underwear when Jerry called him. At least that's how he told me it happened.

What I appreciated was that Barry walked into that locker room for the first time, and before he even addressed the team, he came directly over to me and said I was his bell cow, meaning the leader of the group. I was going to be the guy for the defense. Jimmy did that, too. He made me feel like the focal point, and I respected that.

I told Barry point-blank that I would go through hell for him. We connected immediately. There was definitely a bond between us. Maybe because we both kind of felt like outsiders.

Barry treated me so damn well. We used to ride motorcycles together. He is a funny guy and would tell some of the best jokes I've ever heard. He always stayed engaged, too. I went over to his house, and he introduced his entire family to me. When someone tells you to come over to their house and you meet their family, that's when you know people care about you. That stuff you never forget. I love Coach Switzer very much. I'll do anything for him. My phone could ring this very moment, and if he needs me, I'm driving up to Oklahoma 10 seconds later.

Even though we had lost a bunch of starters via free agency the last two offseasons, we were again expected to win the Super Bowl. No team has ever won three straight to this day, so it's obviously not easy to do. But those were the expectations: win or be labeled a failure. It didn't matter which players we lost or that we had a new coach. And we liked that for the most part. We wanted to win, we wanted the pressure, but with Jimmy gone, everything intensified.

That 1994 team still possessed so much talent. Emmitt was playing at another level, the line was just as solid, and the defense, we again allowed the fewest yards in the entire league while beating up on some quarterbacks. Our 47 sacks were the most we recorded during my time with the Cowboys. I led the team with 12.5 while earning All-Pro honors, and Jim Jeffcoat added eight. Chad Hennings, Tony Tolbert, and that defensive line was definitely the strength of the defense, along with safety Darren Woodson.

The offense took the majority, if not all, of the headlines, but we took immense pride in our group. Statistically speaking, in terms of points and yardage allowed, that was the best four-year run by a defense in Cowboys history. They didn't call us "Doomsday," like the Dallas defenses of the 1960s and 1970s, but trust me, those opposing quarterbacks remember us.

We finished 12–4 that year with each of our four losses by a touchdown or less and won another division title, but our nemesis, my old team, the 49ers, went 13–3 and earned home-field advantage. So for the third straight postseason, the two best teams in the NFL would be playing in the NFC Championship Game, and this one was back at Candlestick Park.

For many of us, like Troy, Emmitt, Michael, myself, this was the most disappointing loss of our careers. Jerry cried afterward. I cried. Hell, I retired. I was done. I couldn't go through anything like that ever again, so after the game, I decided I was a goner. That's the kind of emotional draining that took place during that one afternoon.

The 49ers scored 21 points before a lot of folks watching on television had even finished their first beer. It was crazy. We turned it over a few times, and Barry picked up a few penalties arguing with this one official. But we made a comeback for the ages, and if we had pulled it off, they'd still be writing books about it. And we had a real chance if not for that horrific no-call on Deion Sanders covering Michael. If that's not pass interference, then don't have the rule. Yeah, I'm still bitter.

I still blame myself for that loss. Put that one on me because if I hadn't let Steve Young break out and run a bootleg on my ass, I think we win that game. He was quick, though, a heck of an athlete. Still, it's important for me to say this: the best team won that day. It's difficult for me to say, but it's the truth and needs to be said. On that day, George and Steve got the better of me.

Maybe it comes with growing old, but I tend to regret certain plays more than the actual winning and losing of games. Hey, somebody has to win and somebody has to lose, and on that day at Candlestick, you realize the 49ers were a better team. As hard as we played, and we played as hard as any team I've ever been a part of, when you give up three touchdowns in the first quarter, it's hard to come back. I was more proud that we never gave up than whether we won or lost. The fight, you carry that on for the next year and for the rest of your life. That's one of the great lessons in all of this. We stayed and we fought like our lives were on the line.

That game stands out as much as my five Super Bowl wins. I'm not sure what that says. Barry, that man took more crap than anyone ever has about how he didn't have the pulse of the team and the players tuned him out. Well, guess what? We were killing ourselves in that game. Guys are walking around with limps to this day because of what we gave that day. We fell behind 21–0 on the road. For other teams that's high noon for checking out, but we stayed and fought.

Barry gave one of the best speeches I've ever heard that day, and I'm not a speech guy. He said we would take the kind of effort we gave to our graves and that we should be damn proud of that. After the game in the locker room, I said I was retiring. That's how distressed I was. You know how emotions are running high. That's why they give players 10 or 15 minutes before they talk with the media, so you can let some of that frustration roll off.

It's either you are winning and you want to play forever, or you lose and feel done. That was a low for me. For a football player, for a man, who lives the game like I did, losing to the 49ers, not having a chance to play for three straight Super Bowls, that was devastating.

I overreacted and I knew it. I apologized to my teammates, which was no big thing. I could say sorry when I was wrong. Losing that game was like losing a loved one, like a death, but then with time, you realize this too shall pass.

Also, I always wanted to be productive, contribute something to society and I didn't think I had much to offer off the field, so I wanted to keep playing football for as long as my body would allow.

That was a long season on many fronts. We couldn't go 10 minutes without Jimmy this or Jimmy that. Well, Jimmy couldn't make it work with Jerry or vice versa. Either way, he wasn't there, and we were. The hoopla about Jimmy ended when we lost that NFC Championship Game. There was no more focus or talk among the players about Jimmy after that. It was a long, difficult season, and now we were moving on. We limped into the playoffs and were mentally and physically exhausted.

We decided that from the next minicamp going forward, Barry was our coach. No more excuses. No more what-ifs. The window was closing. We weren't getting any younger and we were losing two or three starters to free agency every time someone scratched their ass. If we were going to win another Super Bowl, it was going to be the 1995 season. Another year of Super Bowl or bust. Only this time, Deion would be our teammate, not on the opposing sideline.

Chapter 8

Triumph and Tragedy

BY THE TIME our training camp started in 1995, there were a lot of new faces. More importantly, the new faces were second-tier replacements for those who had left for more dough via free agency. We were certainly not the same team we were when we won back-to-back Super Bowls. So when Jerry Jones approached me about the possibility of Dallas signing cornerback Deion Sanders, I was thrilled. In the NFC Championship Game a few months earlier, he had covered Michael Irvin really, really well. That didn't happen often. No one was shutting down Michael in his prime, but Deion came the closest.

Thing is, as great as I thought Deion was before we signed him, seeing him play every day really gave me a deeper appreciation for his greatness. I have no idea how many gears he had, but my God, he could run like no one else I've ever seen. He brought a lot of excitement to the team also. He energized me. There could have been a plateau there after not winning the previous season, not being able to become the first team to win three straight Super Bowls. But Deion made sure that didn't happen. He brought energy every day to practice and to the locker room. Wherever Deion was, there was that energy.

Adding Deion was a difference maker for us. We went 12–4 and won the division again, and having him on the team was a big reason why. He was a fun guy to be around. A lot of people assume Deion's a me-first kind of guy, but he isn't. He seemed to get along with everyone; he never big-timed anyone that I saw.

I forget who we were playing, but we were beating them pretty good late in the game and I didn't want to tackle anyone. (As the years went on and my body had completely fallen apart, I wasn't exactly in a rush to tackle someone if the game was in control.) So I took the tight end, threw him, and the ball carrier bounced outside to Deion. The guy didn't have a choice. He had to come up and get in the play. After making the tackle, Deion jumped up and started yelling at me, "I saw you. I saw you. Why are you pulling that shit? I don't want to tackle anyone." He was so mad at me, and I couldn't stop laughing. I was laughing for 10 minutes. He was pissed. Deion wasn't a big fan of having to tackle anyone. Seeing him mad was the best part of the whole deal because you usually can't rattle Deion. He's always the coolest cat in the room.

Before every game Deion would lay his uniform out on the floor in the locker room. I'm talking the jersey, the gloves, the shoes, the bandana, everything. He would meticulously lay it all out in front of his locker. That home locker room at the old Texas Stadium was small, so sometimes I would walk in and kick it out of the way. He didn't like that either. He'd tell me that was bad luck, that I was going to cause the entire team bad luck by doing that. Maybe that's why I kept hurting my back that season because I was kicking his stuff around before games.

Deion is also one of the funniest guys I ever played with. The entire team, not just the defense, talked so much trash to him. There was a lot of fun stuff that season because of Deion. He used to call me "Overbite." He was always busting balls.

And Deion came in at our level. He was already a superstar, but he never acted differently. He talked to everyone, ate with everyone, and joked with everybody in the locker room. He was human. He allowed us to see that human side of him. We didn't see that glamorous side that he has. We saw the real Deion, and it was amazing. I love the dude. You couldn't have a better friend. If Deion asked me to go to the moon, I would because he's not like everybody else where they're always asking you to do something, but then when you ask them, they never show up. Deion will show up and show out, and I love him for that.

I would watch film of offenses playing against us, and it's like people always said: their gameplan was drawing a line down the middle of the field and deciding, *We're not throwing to Deion's side.* Still, the guy was making plays all the time, intercepting passes, and returning them for scores.

He told me that he counted in his head—1,001, 1,002, 1,003—and he said if the ball wasn't out by then, it was going to be a sack or the quarterback was going to throw a bad pass. So he would break off his man and then would play center field. Most of his interceptions didn't come on balls thrown at him. The ball was thrown in someone else's direction, but he would just break off, anticipate it, catch it, and take it to the house.

That high-step that he did, like a Heisman pose in rhythm, kids are still doing it today. I see girls doing it after scoring goals in my daughter's soccer games. You know what I can't believe to this day is that he would start that high-step stuff like 30 yards out, and no one ever caught him. I never, ever recall seeing Deion get caught from behind.

We were still a heck of a football team that season—just not invincible. We lost Pro Bowl offensive lineman Mark Stepnoski through free agency and we almost lost one of the best I've ever gone up against in right tackle Erik Williams. Like lost for real.

"Big E" crashed his Mercedes 600SL the season before on October 24, 1994 and missed the remainder of the year. He was messed up real good. It's a miracle he survived. If you saw that car, you would have been certain he died. He somehow came back, but he was never close to the same player. That screwed him up big time. I went to the hospital the day after the accident. I walked in his room, saw him, and started crying. I had to walk out, I had to leave. It was just…damn, it was bad. Tony Tolbert and I went in to see him, and it was just horrific.

The rookie who replaced Erik in 1994 and became a permanent starter was the massive Larry Allen. This guy was otherworldly. He could lift like 800 pounds. His first practice—at least the first time we were on the field at the same time, as I wasn't practicing much at this point because of my back—I'm talking trash, telling him he's a rookie piece of filth and all that kind of stuff. The first snap, the very first snap, that dude picked me up and tossed me like a rag doll. Like in one motion, he just hooked and launched me. I slowly stood up and walked over to our offensive line coach, Hudson Houck, and said, "Coach, you have one heck of a player there."

That was my last time talking crap to Larry Allen. He ended up being a first-ballot Pro Football Hall of Fame selection. We'd be watching film of guys going up against him, and they would just quit. I guess kind of like me with Jackie Slater. Hey man, I'm telling you, that stuff hurts.

Speaking of hurt, my back was a mess. I am going to talk about injuries and concussions more extensively in another chapter, but there's no way of telling the story of the 1995 season without mentioning my back. The pain became so unbearable, and my mobility had become so limited, that in December I finally succumbed to surgery. Everyone figured it was season-ending. I was definitely going to miss the last three regular-season games, but I was determined to come back if we advanced in the playoffs. This wasn't my first back surgery, and it wouldn't be my last. In terms of football, especially a pass rusher with wear and tear, I was an old man of 32 on the morning of Super Bowl XXX.

Yes, it was the morning of the Super Bowl, and my ass was playing, trying to become the first player in the history of the league to win five. I made a commitment to my teammates. When I left the team to have the surgery, I told them, "Get me to the Super Bowl, and I'll be on the field." This was as important a game as we ever played together because winning back-to-back championships doesn't constitute a dynasty. Winning three of four, now that's a dynasty.

And I think we all kind of knew that this was the end of the rodeo. More players would be leaving, and, honestly, after the pressure and stress of that season, I think we were ready for the conclusion.

I was all worried about trying to somehow take the field in the NFC Championship Game because we all assumed the 49ers would once again be our opponent. Instead, the upstart Green Bay Packers with quarterback Brett Favre knocked out San Francisco and gave us all we could handle and then some. No one really talks about that game, but it was great football. We were actually trailing entering the fourth quarter before eventually winning 38–27. It sucked having to watch and not play. Still, I knew my back had only one game left max and I was betting on my teammates in hopes of playing in another Super Bowl.

It paid off. We would face the Pittsburgh Steelers at Sun Devil Stadium in Tempe, Arizona. I honestly didn't think I would be able to play, even a few days before, because all the discs in my back had disintegrated. Like a few of my teammates, I was also battling the flu. Yeah, I was a mess. The fusion surgery wasn't a cakewalk either. They ended up putting gauges in to lift my spine up and then they put rods in there. That was the most difficult of the 10 surgeries, just brutal. To this day people are always asking me, "Was it worth it?"

I look at them like they're crazy. Maybe they never played the game—or any game. Hell yes, it was worth it. And I would do it again and again, make those same decisions, endure the pain because I love football so much. The game has done a whole lot more for me than I could do for it. For the game and my teammates, the pain was more than worth being able to take the field.

That morning, my phone rings. It was Ronnie Lott. He talked about all the great players who have won four Super Bowls—all these Steelers —Terry Bradshaw, "Mean" Joe Greene, Franco Harris—and then some of my teammates with San Francisco—Joe Montana, Ronnie himself, Keena Turner, Eric Wright, and Matt Millen. It was a memorable conversation for me. Here I was, this kid from Gladys with a chance to do something no one else had. That was meaningful stuff. I have always appreciated that phone call.

We're in the locker room before the game, and Coach Switzer walks in. He walked by Michael, Troy, all those guys and he comes to me, smiles, and says, "You're my bell cow today." It was the same thing he told me the first time we met. For people to believe in me, they get everything I have, especially at that point in my life when I never thought people cared or believed in me. And Coach Switzer was real. He was the most real coach I ever had. He didn't tell us what to do. You knew what you were supposed to do. Live up and do it. Some guys couldn't.

Let me tell you something, the Steelers came to play that day. They really should have beat us. Their quarterback, Neil O'Donnell, threw three interceptions, two to Larry Brown, one of our cornerbacks and a good guy. One of those was a Christmas present. On the other one, I hit him as he was throwing, which redirected the throw. I was able to register a sack, too. In the kind of pain I was in, it felt great to make a contribution in what would be my last Super Bowl. Although the final score was 27–17, we were fortunate to win.

I have one motto in life: if I put my feet on the field, then I'm not hurt. I played most of the year with a herniated disc and I played the year before with a herniated disc, so you know, pain-wise, there was no problem. I could compartmentalize the pain because I wouldn't take pain pills and stuff. The greatest part of it was that I was able to go out and not only play, but also be effective, be there for my teammates. I always told the defensive line that I would never forsake them because we were a brotherhood. I could never let those guys down.

I was so exhausted afterward that I didn't even celebrate. I might have drank a beer in the locker room, I don't recall. The magnitude of the moment didn't really hit me for a few days. I don't understand why my psyche is like that, but it's always been that way. I woke up one morning later that week and I just kind of nodded to no one and said, "Wow, I've done something that no football player has ever accomplished." And even today, no player has won five. It's just me.

I was a pain in the ass to my teammates and coaches over the years, I know that. I think on that day, though, having returned from the back surgery and playing when the doctors told me not to, I hope I was able to inspire them, show them how driven I was to help them in any way I could. There is always sacrifice for success, and that's the most sacrifice, physically speaking, I have ever given. My back is sloped and jacked up to this day because I played in that Super Bowl. I'm incredibly proud of winning five Super Bowls. I understand that will be the first line of my obituary and I'm okay with that. In terms of being a football player at any level, never mind the NFL, the objective should be winning. And my teams won a lot of games.

There were several times when I thought seriously about retiring. I even announced it a few times, including that previous December before having the back surgery. In terms of retiring, I guess I was Favre before Favre. Looking back, my back just wasn't strong enough to return in 1996, but I did anyway. Camp was a train wreck. I was just jogging one day at practice and felt a twinge in my back. It was never the same after that. The pain injections on Mondays were no longer helping. I could only play so many snaps. I wasn't close to the player I was even the previous season. I played five games and mustered just six tackles and a sack. That would have been a decent game for me the previous 10 years.

The lone highlight came in beating the Miami Dolphins and their new head coach, Jimmy Johnson. We beat them good, too, 29–10. After the game I made my way across the field, but instead of shaking hands with the man who did so much for my career, I was typical petulant Charles, saying, "How about them fuckin' Cowboys now?"

I've since apologized to Jimmy. He's been good to me. It was one of those in-the-moment things. The following week, on November 3, I played in a home loss to the Philadelphia Eagles. Ricky Watters, their running back, was coming toward me. He was going to throw a block at my legs. I spun, trying to avoid it and in the process was then going to explode toward the quarterback. But there was no explosion left, and pain went down my spine in ways I can't really explain. It felt like fireworks were in there, and I went down. Watching the replay, my body was going in three different directions, and I just kept spinning. When I hit the ground, I knew that was it. I told Coach Switzer a few minutes later that I was done. He understood and gave me a hug, saying, "You left it on the field Charles. You always left it on the field."

That was my last game for the Cowboys.

I had signed a four-year, $12 million deal in the summer of 1995 and I guess I came back more out of loyalty for Jerry Jones and Barry for having faith in me. And again, I didn't really have a post-football plan. After yet another back surgery a few weeks after that Philly game, though, the time had arrived. My body couldn't play any more football. My sorry ass couldn't even pee without having to hold on to a wall to stabilize myself. To celebrate my retirement, I had more back surgery.

There wasn't much time for a transition or for me to mourn about retiring because my daughter, Brianna, was diagnosed with leukemia on May 28, 1997. That day was terrible. It was easily the worst day of my life. She was three years old. After that, every day the focus for Karen and me was entirely on trying to save her life. That's the toughest thing I've ever experienced because I thought with all of my money and connections that I could save her. Her father should be able to save her life, but I couldn't. We couldn't find a bone marrow transplant who was an exact match.

It drove me crazy. I was so angry. I was angry at the world. I was a mess, drinking a lot and doing other stuff, bad stuff. Football was completely and totally irrelevant to me at that time. I wasn't watching any of it. I just wanted to save my daughter's life. I had a lot of people step up in trying to aid us. When they all step up and rally behind you in trying to help you save your daughter, that's when you know you have friends. It meant a whole lot to me, especially at a time when I was falling apart emotionally.

Brianna would always run and jump into my arms when I returned from a trip. I was in Virginia and flew home to Dallas. It was at the airport—I remember this so vividly—and she slowly walked over. I picked her up, and she let out this cry that almost broke my heart. That was the first time we knew something was wrong. We rushed her to the pediatrician, who looked at her and immediately called for an ambulance to the Children's Medical Center of Dallas. They didn't tell us anything, though in retrospect, they were focused on my baby girl like they should have been. I must have driven 110 miles per hour to that hospital. That was the toughest battle of my life. There was nothing I could do. I was helpless.

They told us at the hospital that she had acute lymphoid leukemia, and that it would take a medical miracle to save her. Karen and I would go into the hospital and hold her down while they did spinal taps, and she would just scream. My three-year-old girl was screaming, and I couldn't stop it. That's when my true colors came out. I became a coward. I ran to the bottle. I started doing recreational drugs. I just could not cope with the reality.

They tried several experimental procedures with spinal taps and platelets, all that stuff. It was draining for the entire family, including my two older children because their parents were almost never around anymore. Or at least we were spending the majority of our time at the hospital. We searched the world for a donor but to no avail. Part of the problem, well, a big part of the problem was that only 7 percent of the three million or so donors at the time were black. And a matching donor is almost always found in the same racial or ethnic group when a match isn't found within the immediate family, which was the case with us. It was a nightmare.

Thanks to Jerry Jones and his family, we organized the biggest bone marrow drive ever. Some 2,000 people came to Texas Stadium, but more than 90 percent of them were caucasian. Minorities just don't show up for that stuff, I guess. It's frustrating that you cannot get them to understand that we have to help each other. When I go back through my life, it was almost always white folks who helped me out. You have to understand that my world growing up was segregated, so you become a product of your environment. When I came into the NFL, I might have had some racist views even after James Madison, which made no sense.

So one day, in the midst of my career, I'm sitting there, and somebody asked me to name the people who had helped me over the course of my life. I started naming everyone, and most of them were white. And now here again when my daughter was sick, most were white. It's the life lessons that mold the man, and that one was pretty valuable for me.

It's all about family, and when mine was struggling, Jerry really took the time to care and give a damn. He was instrumental in trying to find donors, facilitating the best healthcare, holding charity events to raise money, writing a check himself. I'll never forget that. I am so respectful and grateful for everything Jerry did in helping my little girl. I didn't think Brianna would survive because we couldn't find a donor. Karen kept the family's spirits up; she was so strong. Playing football is easy compared with the pain we were dealing with. There is nothing like seeing a child in pain.

We were in the cancer unit of the hospital for a long time, and in that time, they would come ask me to sit with other kids and sign autographs, whatever I could do to help. I'd make a call to one of my former teammates if he was the kid's favorite player. I did what I could. And Brianna made friends with a lot of the kids there, too. This was their world for so long. Outside of visitors, the only people they saw were the doctors, nurses, and the other kids in the hospital.

I would ask the doctors or Karen, "How is this kid doing that I spent some time with last week?" And there were many instances where the answer was, "Well, they had to amputate their leg, or the cancer has spread," and some passed away. Some four-year-old kid with a world of dreams and innocence was leaving us to become an angel in heaven.

This crap was grossly unfair. I was falling apart more and more, just drinking alone and cursing the world. I was in the darkest of places.

I guess it's about control. I thought I was in control. That's the whole deal. At James Madison I was in control of changing my life, working hard for an education, building a life with Karen. Then I made a lot of money in the NFL, which allowed me more control. I could buy nice stuff for my mother and Karen and my kids. I could buy Harley-Davidson motorcycles. I was in control. And when Brianna was diagnosed, I figured I could go out and find someone to save my daughter's life, but I couldn't. I wasn't in control. It broke me down. It broke me as a man.

At that moment I dropped to my knees and surrendered to God. I left it in his hands. I wasn't happy, but if nothing else, I admitted to myself that I wasn't in control—of my daughter's health and really myself. Ronnie Lott helped me as much as anyone with my drinking and depression during this time. Ronnie and Karen were there, like for so much of my life.

I slowly came out of my funk and began working with the Marrow Foundation in Washington, D.C. The first study I read said that as recently as 1994 only 15 percent of black people who needed a bone marrow transplant could expect to find one. Those numbers have greatly increased since, but that was scary. I traveled the country, ran fund-raisers, spoke at every college that would have me, and sat on the Marrow Foundation's board of directors. I grew so frustrated with those unwilling to just donate blood, never mind bone marrow.

In early 1998 Karen told me she was pregnant. That gave us a chance. On October 25, 1998, she gave birth to Madison, whose bone marrow was a 100 percent match. To save my daughter, I had to give up, I had to relinquish control, and God took over. After the procedure, Brianna went into remission, which meant mostly just giving her IVs at night.

I do a lot of children's charity work to this day. I just visit hospitals and talk with the kids. I was doing this fund-raiser at a Dallas hotel a few years ago, and they were showing this film about how a lot of young kids diagnosed with leukemia don't survive. They were showing these beautiful little children in their hospital beds, and then we found out that they didn't make it. I was crying so hard, and every time I think of it, I still cry inside because that could have been my daughter. It drives me crazy to think about. If anyone calls asking me to do an event for kids, I'm there.

Ever since our scare, when I see other parents lose their daughter, it's just as emotional for me as it would have been for me losing Brianna. The pain is so deep and real. Brianna has been healthy to this day and graduated from James Madison in the spring of 2016 with a nursing degree. I couldn't be more proud of her.

A couple of months after Madison was born, right before Christmas, my phone rang. It was Bill Walsh, who was back working in the front office of the San Francisco 49ers. They were headed for the postseason, and he was wondering if I could join them. Not as a spectator, not like sitting next to him in some suite, or even as like a volunteer assistant coach. No, he was asking me to return to the field as a player.

I was a fat load, like 280 pounds, and hadn't exercised since Brianna was diagnosed. I was a week or so from turning 35 years old, and my back still ached. This certainly didn't sound like an appealing proposition. It was Bill Walsh, though. I couldn't say no to Bill, so I was going to answer the call. My playing days weren't over quite yet. At the time, in my wildest dreams, I couldn't imagine that I would soon be playing in one of the most memorable playoff games in NFL history.

Chapter 9

Back in San Fran

I DON'T REMEMBER there being many phone calls from NFL teams after I retired. The word around the league was that my body was toast, especially my back. And it was. Let's be honest, teams barely wanted to deal with me when I was one of the best pass rushers on the planet. Now that I was old and a mere shell of myself, I'm sure the thought process was to look elsewhere. And again, I was retired. There was no reason to think I wanted to come back.

The 49ers, now coached by Steve Mariucci, finished 12–4 in 1998 with one of the top offenses in the league and were still led by Steve Young and Jerry Rice. Some guys don't age as quickly as others. So Bill Walsh called and asked if I have one more game in me. Hopefully a few, actually, if the team advanced. You're probably wondering how I was able to bury the hatchet with the 49ers after leaving on such bad terms. I mean they were even willing to trade me to the Cowboys, one of their rivals, just to get rid of my ass. The reason for the reconciliation was 100 percent Bill Walsh. He was now back running the show, and whatever problems I had with the 49ers—or they had with me—it was never with Walsh, whom I respect so much. I could never say no to that man.

So I flew out there to San Francisco and worked out. I was 40 pounds heavier than I was for the last game I played in the NFL more than two years ago and like 75 pounds more than when I came into the league. I was a big boy—chubby and out of shape. The workout went fine, and then they did the physical. The doctor said, "Oh, my God, your back is a disaster." *I know, Doc, I know.* I really didn't think they were going to pass me. The doctor couldn't believe how banged up I was. Somehow, some way, though, maybe in one of those wink-wink deals, they passed me.

I felt like I could still play. As a player, you always think you have one more game, one more season in you. It's the mentality. Bill taught us that. He would say, "At the end of the game, you should always be able to play another down. You should never be tired enough where you can't play another snap. You should always have enough in the tank to help your team with one more effort." He was brilliant and he was always pushing us mentally. His teams always played smart.

With Bill's words in my mind, there I found myself at Candlestick Park on January 3, 1999, playing the Green Bay Packers in a wild-card game. And what a game it was. I even made some plays, most importantly putting a hit on Brett Favre as he threw what would be an interception. Those are the plays that don't show up on the stat sheet.

I was happy to make a contribution. They scored, we scored; it was back and forth. And then Steve threw a gorgeous pass into double coverage to Terrell Owens with eight seconds left and we won 30–27. "T.O." was hit by both defenders and hung on to the football. That was a heck of a game.

I actually started the following week and played more snaps, but we lost to the Atlanta Falcons 20–18. Again, and this is definitely starting to sound like a broken record, but that should have been it. It was time for Charles to go home. But they talked me into another season, though. I lost a little weight and tried running some in the offseason, but my back was still bothering me. They limited my snaps, and I actually played in all 16 games, finishing with three sacks.

Yeah, three sacks in 16 games. It was not exactly the Pro Bowl performances of my younger days. I couldn't lose enough weight to regain any quickness; it was all smoke and mirrors that season. The game had passed me by, and you know what? It hurt. Like so many athletes, I had to learn the hard way. I didn't have another game or another season in me. I learned the hard way that I didn't.

At one point—this is a true story, too—I went up to Coach Walsh's office and tried giving him back the money they paid me. Thank God, he didn't take it, and I was able to spend a lot of time with him that season. I didn't really have a desire to return. For me, it was just Coach Walsh asking for a favor. He was always so good to me. It was an honor being able to say yes to him—for anything. After that 1999 season, though, it was definitely time to retire again. And for good.

I enjoyed a lot of that last season—outside of us completely falling apart and finishing 4–12. There was a funny story from that first week of practice. They didn't make me do training camp, so this was back at our headquarters. We're doing some kind of scrimmage thing, and a guard pulled around and hit me. I walked off the field right up to Bill's office and said, "This hurts. I'm going home. Football never hurt like this before." And he was laughing. Every bone in my body is shouting for help, I'm all red and sore, and Bill's laughing. I should have stayed home.

In terms of practicing the rest of the season, I did a lot of teaching and showing others how to watch film. None of that hitting crap. That's for those younger guys. That's probably why it wasn't demoralizing for me because I became a teacher. I was able to tell guys, okay, you need to do this, this, and this, and you'll be a better pass rusher or better against the run. I was kind of like a glorified assistant coach who could play a little bit at the same time, mostly on third-down passing situations. And I was quite happy with my limited role of 15, maybe 20 plays a game.

We had a lot of veteran guys when I returned to San Francisco, and we stayed on Terrell's ass pretty good. Back then, he wasn't the way he ended up. He was a pretty cool dude. He and I used to play dominoes for hours and just make fun of each other about the shape of our heads, our facial features, etc. We'd just tool on each other.

I think for T.O., when some of those veteran guys left, he just grew into that personality or persona that we all now know. He was a hell of a player, just a physical specimen like no wide receiver I have ever seen. He was cut from his feet all the way up, and there was nothing he couldn't do on the field. The man would block his ass off, too. He wasn't one of those wide receivers who didn't like the physicality of the game. I've always liked the guy, though there were times when you would wonder what he was thinking. Then again, there were many times when others were wondering what the hell I was thinking, too.

Chapter 10

Pain and Gain

WITH MY PLAYING career finished, there was some thought that the aches and pains would diminish. Not so much. The physical abuse that most of us football players do to our bodies, that stays with us for a lifetime. I can honestly say that a day hasn't passed since I retired where some part of my body doesn't hurt. Know what, though? My back and my knees aren't my biggest worry, though limping around and having to use handicap license plates in your 40s sucks big-time. That's for senior citizens.

I have post-concussion syndrome. I'm not entirely sure what the medical definition of that is—likely something about headaches and dizziness. All I know is my short-term memory is awful. The headaches are still there, too, mostly in my eyes. Those were a lot worse during my playing days, never more so than during my rookie season.

Even worse is just not being able to remember anything. That's obviously some pretty serious stuff. I used to remember everything. I wasn't born with book smarts. That took a lot of hard work at James Madison, but I could always remember stuff. More than anything, my memory and my conditioning were why I was successful as a football player. And now, my memory is a cruel reminder of all those head-to-head collisions.

Some days I find myself thinking about what took place just an hour before and wondering if I will remember it the next day. A lot of the time I won't. I'll write some of it down and when I read it, I'll be like, no, I don't remember that. It's sad and frustrating at the same time. There are occasions when someone pushes me on an answer, one they just assume I'll know because it's in reference to something that just happened earlier in the week, and I can't do it. Again, though, and I'll stress this again and again—there are no regrets.

In January of 2016, the great Commonwealth of Virginia passed a resolution recognizing me for honorably representing my home state during my NFL career. They did a little ceremony for me, and I was talking with governor Terry McAuliffe. We were just making small talk, and he obviously saw how I was walking, or limping to be more accurate, and he said, "So, was it worth it?"

I said, "Yes, sir. It was definitely worth it. I was poor. You see that lady right there? You see how she's dressed up all nice. That's my momma. You see my brothers over there? All of their kids either went to college or are currently attending college. There's nobody holding them back anymore. So yes, 100 times over, it was worth it for me."

Now, I wish I'd have known a little more during my career. I wish they were doing some of the stuff then that they are now. I'm sure every player feels that way, going back to the early days of the game. The league has done a great job in turning that around. A lot of the safety policies that they have put in place of late have dramatically lessened the physical risks.

The concussion protocol, that's a game-changer right there. I think we would all be floored if we saw the number of players who had remained in games with concussions over the years. The number would be in the millions. That's not only in the NFL either. Colleges, high schools, Pop Warner, whatever the level, we were all playing with concussions for a long time. We called them stingers for the most part, but looking back, I'm guessing a lot of those were concussions.

I do think the biggest remaining problem is with the wide receivers running downfield and not watching for those safeties. The ball is thrown up there, the safety is flying in full speed, and the receivers don't try to cover up before that lick. That bothers me a lot. That's going to bother me until my last breath. They need to figure that out. I know there's that defenseless receiver rule now, but they are still taking some ridiculous hits to the head. That's a problem.

People ask me all the time about whether they should allow their sons to play football. I tell them yes. My son, C.J., played in high school and at the University of Texas at El Paso (UTEP). Look, football is a great sport. Sure, it can be dangerous, but it doesn't have to be as dangerous as it sometimes is. All kids have to do is stop looking at the ground. *Do not look at the ground.* If they see grass—I'm talking youth ball to the pros—you only have to bend your neck just a little, and it's a concussion. I tell this to guys all the time.

When you see players being concussed, the majority of the time they have their head looking down at the ground. In that position you have no strength, no balance, nothing. On the occasions that I was knocked out, they came when I put my head down and was trying to cut the pulling guard or something like that, and my head hit his knee.

I tell kids every chance I get that it's okay for the other team to get a first down. It really is. If it's third and 1, you don't have to make the stop by any and all means necessary. Those days are behind us. Hit them up top and drive your legs. Don't go launching yourself over the pile, helmet first. The helmet isn't a weapon. It's not an extension of your body. It's for protection, not to inflict pain and suffering.

I'm an ambassador for football. When they need somebody to go talk to high school kids or some youth team about the game, I'm there. Call me up, and I'm there that day. I want to help and give back because I love the game, and the game changed my world. Oftentimes, though, we have fundamental differences in teaching how to tackle. I focus on not seeing the grass. They want me to focus on head up, look at the chest, that stuff. I have to use whatever it's going to take to teach this kid what I want, what's going to protect him. I don't visit as many schools and teams as I used to because they want me focusing on the technique, and I don't think that's the biggest issue. It's where a player's eyes are, what they are looking at.

Another problem, too, in terms of why players are always suffering injuries and concussions is that they're out of shape. Then when a team goes no-huddle, you have guys reaching instead of engaging, and that's when their legs are taken out. There's a difference between being injured while going hard—and I was hurt a ton just with two guys going hard against each other—and injuries where one of the guys is just in the trash. The ball is on the other side of the field, and a guy just stops while the other is still pushing, still finishing out the play. Your foot gets caught under, and boom, you're hurt.

They don't teach guys to keep their feet moving and get off the block. One of my frustrations is that the little things aren't being taught anymore. It's not being taught in college and it's not being taught in high schools. All they seem to have time for is teaching them how to line up and go after one another. It's not about teaching them skills and fundamentals.

I'm not trying to sound like, "Hey, get off my lawn," and "The game was so much better in my day." I'm not that guy. I just want football to last forever, and at the same time, for players to have a better quality of life after their careers. I don't want them to end up like me. You read about all these former players passing away, and they find CTE (chronic traumatic encephalopathy) from too many blows to the head, and you read about all of these former players with dementia. It's not only football either. It's other sports like boxing, hockey, other contact sports.

It's scary stuff.

Like just about every other former NFL player, more than 5,000 of us, I'm a part of the concussion lawsuit against the league. We settled in 2015 for at least $900 million, but the judge came back and said that wasn't enough. Who knows when that will finally be settled, but I just hope it helps take care of some of the guys who are really struggling. I told NFL commissioner Roger Goodell that I would rather they just put the money into our pension. That way, if by some miracle I live to be 90 years old, I always have some money in there.

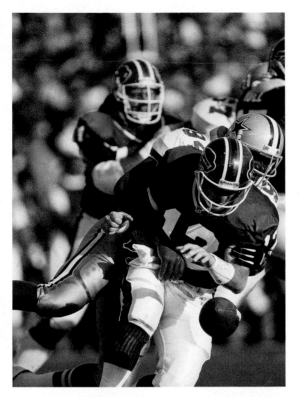

(Left) I strip the ball from Buffalo Bills quarterback Jim Kelly during our 52–17 win in Super Bowl XXVII. (USA TODAY Sports Images)

(Bottom) Despite undergoing back fusion surgery in December, I sack Pittsburgh Steelers quarterback Neil O'Donnell on January 28, 1996, during Super Bowl XXX to earn my fifth ring. (USA TODAY Sports Images)

I pose with four of the Lombardi Trophies. I am the only NFL player to have won five of them. (Dallas Cowboys)

(Top) During gamedays I always had a look of intensity. (Dallas Cowboys)

(Right) I played through multiple injuries during my 13 years in the NFL. But even though I'm paying the price now, I have no regrets. (Dallas Cowboys)

I pose with my family and friends after my retirement from the Dallas Cowboys. I was sure that I was done playing in the NFL. (Dallas Cowboys)

(Top) The 49ers announce my re-signing. Why did I come out of retirement? Because Bill Walsh (left) asked me to join head coach Steve Mariucci's team, and I would do anything for Bill. (AP Images)

(Bottom) I hit Green Bay Packers quarterback Brett Favre to force an interception during a 1999 wild-card game. We won this epic contest on a last-second touchdown pass from Steve Young to Terrell Owens. (AP Images)

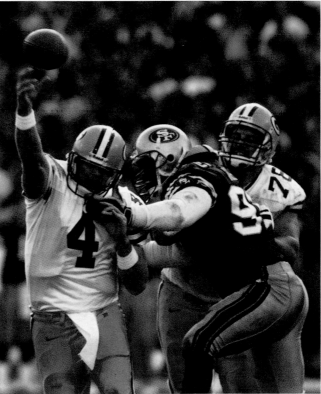

I pose with my presenter—a great owner and friend—Edward DeBartolo Jr. during the 2015 induction ceremony at the Pro Football Hall of Fame. (AP Images)

During a Hall of Fame ceremony at the halftime of a 2015 Monday Night Football *game between the Minnesota Vikings and San Francisco 49ers, I pose with 49ers legends, including Steve Young, Joe Montana, Jerry Rice, Ronnie Lott, and the DeBartolo family.* (USA TODAY Sports Images)

Between the first and second quarters of a home game against the Seattle Seahawks during the 2015 season, Pro Football Hall of Fame president and executive director David Baker and Dallas Cowboys owner Jerry Jones present me with my Hall of Fame ring. (Dallas Cowboys)

I show off the Hall of Fame ring to Jerry Jones, a man who always had my back, during a 2015 ceremony. (Dallas Cowboys)

*(Top) My son, Charles Jr.
stands back while Madison
(held by Karen), Brianna
(holding number), me, and
Princess pose at a charity
race.* (Charles Haley)

*(Bottom) During Christmas
time I hang out with my
family. From left to right
are: Brianna, Karen, me,
Madison, Princess, and
Charles Jr.* (Charles Haley)

I can only talk about my situation, and when I try to think back, I can't remember the majority of my past. Even writing this book, there weren't a lot of specific memories from football games. It was easy to remember things from growing up, high school, and college. That's more long-term memory. It's the stuff from the last 20 or so years that becomes more and more fuzzy. Most of the football stories that remain in my mind are the ones I'm always talking about. We all have go-to stories that we tell when we meet people. So those are almost engrained in my head, like memorizing your lines in a movie or something.

But there's so much that I just don't remember, and I can only imagine that it's going to get worse and not better. My future is going to include less and less of my past. I can't remember the names of the doctors who delivered my kids. Never mind the doctors, I really don't remember much about the birth of my last three kids. I tend to remember stuff that I wish I could forget, like the tragic stuff. I can remember everything people have done to me, at least how I perceived it in my mind. Yet, I barely remember any of the crap I did to other people. Maybe I don't want to remember that. Maybe that's just a fail-safe for me.

When I see someone, a lightbulb comes on, and I can remember anything negative they did to me. But if they mention, well, Charles you did this to me or said this, I don't know what they're talking about. I guess that's selective memory as much as memory loss. I guess I have both. I would love to remember more about the good times spent with Karen and my kids. They might mention a story about this time we went to the playground or threw the ball around, and I'll have no idea.

In terms of lifespan, I don't know how long I'll live and I don't worry about it. I'm not an idiot. I know there's a chance I'm not sitting around 30 years from now telling stories about the old days. My body has been abused in many ways. I just don't want to be a burden to my kids. That's the only thing that really matters to me on that front. The league told us that we need to have a power of attorney just in case dementia or whatever sets in where you can't remember who you are. You need to have somebody who can make those decisions for you, and I have that in place.

There is a lot of stuff the league is doing for former players, but the problem is the information is not being communicated so that the players understand it all. I think the big next step is settling the damn lawsuit, so both sides can move on as partners more than adversaries.

I know owners like Jerry Jones and the York family with the 49ers, along with Eddie DeBartolo, I know those kinds of people all want to help former players. No one will ever, ever know how many times Jerry and Mr. D have reached into their pockets to take care of their guys. Those stories usually aren't told, but I personally know of countless incidents.

A lot of NFL players, I guess athletes in general, they don't know how to deal with money. I want guys to live a good life, a long life, a prosperous life. Don't be wasting money on jewelry or these leeches, these inner-circle guys, or whatever they are called nowadays. Take care of yourself and your family. I may have spent a little more than I should have during my playing career, but it was almost always on my family, buying my mother nice clothes, buying Karen something, though she would usually return it and say we didn't need that stuff. Outside of coaching there's not much of a second career for a lot of NFL guys, so save your money. Think big picture.

I am truly blessed because I have a lot of people calling me, meeting me, offering me a job to maybe sign some autographs, make an appearance, whatnot. I don't have to go knock on doors begging for work so I can pay the bills. I'm also fortunate on that front because there's not much I could do anyway these days. Now, I don't want anyone feeling sorry for Charles. I'm just telling it like it is. I knew the deal going in. I definitely have to limit my activities. I don't do anything where I could bump heads with someone. The most I really do is plant my flowers, mow my grass, little things like that. I don't put myself in the danger zone anymore. No cardio for me. I can't jog or anything. Hell, I can barely walk sometimes; that can be a struggle.

Know how they ask you in the hospital what your level of pain is on a scale of one through 10? I'm always at a six, seven, or eight. Like every day, 24 hours. I had surgery in the fall of 2015 because my knees were hurting so bad. That killed me. I mean, I can't explain how painful it was. I think I cried for three days, it was so painful. I could barely speak, that's how much pain I was in. I hurt worse after the surgery than before, though eventually, over time, my knees became a little better. Honestly, this is from a guy who has endured multiple fusion back surgeries, and that knee surgery hurt more. I'm always going to hurt, though.

Let's see if we can assemble the official list of injuries and surgeries. We might need another book for this. Seriously, I walk through airport security, and alarms in the Pentagon start going off. That's how much metal is inside of me. But here's a rundown of my serious injuries:

- So there were the headaches and migraines during my first season with the 49ers from that first concussion in the preseason. Actually, the headaches have been off and on since then. Those never stop.
- And then I had a neck stinger that first season, too. That's why I always wore a neck roll. Ronnie Lott came from about 20 yards back and slapped me upside the head after a sack. That was my first stinger. I still love him, but that hurt. My arm went limp. But I made a big play, and that's the way Ronnie is. He gets excited. I would always mess with him in the locker room when I was putting that neck roll on, "Hey man, this is because of you."

- My first knee injury came that rookie season, too. I had six knee surgeries during my career—three on each knee. Then the surgery on both in 2015, so that's eight total. My knees are shot. It doesn't help being a big guy either. There are great-grandmothers out there who could probably beat me in a 40-yard dash right now.

- I tore my rotator cuff early one year, too, like in the third or fourth game of the season and played the rest of the year in a harness. Then I had surgery on that.

- Then there was the elbow surgery. That nerve we call a funny bone, they took that out and reattached it or something; that's how they explained it. I'm like the bionic man minus the $6 million and the intelligence.

- We can't forget the back. My back has been my nemesis. I've had four back surgeries, including three microdiscectomies, which is the surgical removal of herniated disc material that was pressing on a nerve root or the spinal cord. The fourth was a four-level back fusion, which sucks as much as it sounds like it would. They put three intervertebral fusion cages in to lift my spine up because it had collapsed.

Know what though? We had to play to get paid. No one is paying the guy on injured reserve year after year. Like I said, I tore my rotator cuff and kept playing. Through all of those back surgeries with the Cowboys, I kept playing. I missed 12 regular-season games during my first 10 years in the league and, including the postseason, I was on the field for 167 of the 181 times my teams played. I even played all 16 games in that final season with San Francisco when I was old and fat.

Most players with my back condition would have taken a year off, likely after we won that last Super Bowl with Jimmy following the 1993 season, but life is short. When I look at it as an athlete, opportunities come knocking only once in a lifetime, and you need to step up. That was my mind-set. My thought was: I have a chance to win another Super Bowl, so let's have some surgery, put my ass back together again, and I'll deal with the pain. It's all about what we're willing to endure, and I could take a lot of punishment.

So again, my activity now consists of very little. I do some exercises they gave me to strengthen my knees, but if it starts to feel like it's going to hurt, I have to stop. I don't do pain that well anymore. I've just been dealing with it for so long. I can't golf, I can't do anything that makes me twist.

My quality of life is great, don't get me wrong. I'm just not able to do the things other men in their 50s can do. I used to love running and working out. I can't do that. Maybe I can go for a bike ride here and there, but that hurts, too. Every once in a while, when I'm feeling good, I take my dogs for a walk. That's a big day for me, walking the dogs. And then I hurt for a week.

I also wanted to talk a little about pain medicine. There have been reports of me taking a whole bunch of pills, I guess mostly Vicodin, during my playing days. That's not true. I took injections on Mondays, but honestly, the pain was so bad that by the time I walked out of the building, the effects were already wearing off.

My issue with pain meds is that if I took them to numb the injury, I wouldn't know whether I had reinjured myself. I went out there and I compartmentalized my pain, which helped me bring out my violence. You need to go places within yourself to become this violent football player. You need to find the rage. Pain was one of the ways I did that. Always try and turn a negative into a positive.

My injuries were my weakness, but I would try and make that my strength. There was one game in particular where this was the case. When I was with Dallas, we were playing the Washington Redskins, and Brian Mitchell, a running back, a strong guy, hit me in my hip in the first quarter, and my back popped. I lie down on the ground, and those guys are high-fiving. I'm lying there and I looked up to God. I said, "God, just give me strength." Then I played the rest of the first half and made some plays. I think I even had a sack.

The pain, though, really kicked in when the second quarter ended. The adrenalin wore off. My teammates, Tony Tolbert and Leon Lett, had to help me into the locker room. I couldn't even walk myself. I could see the sadness in their eyes because they knew that I was really hurt. I thought my career was finished. I couldn't go back out for the second half. I was in the shower by myself crying because the pain was so immense. I really thought it was over.

I used that pain, though. I used that pain as my motivation to play again the following week. I did my therapy and I worked hard during the week, thinking about those guys high-fiving while I was lying there. The human body has this amazing ability to recover, especially if you are willing to push your limitations, or what you thought those limitations were. That's why I didn't mess around with pain pills. I wanted to feel the pain, use that as my motivation. And that following week, I was back on the field.

Chapter 11

Living Bipolar

F. SCOTT FITZGERALD famously wrote that there are no second acts in American lives. Well, that certainly hasn't been the case with me. I have very much enjoyed my second act, which began after I was properly diagnosed with bipolar disorder. I'm not exactly sure when I became bipolar. It's not one of those diseases you are born with. I mean, I always felt different, but it's rarely found in children, so who knows? Maybe I was one of those rare cases. When I was fighting everyone and lighting fires as a kid, maybe mental illness was a factor. I honestly do not know, and there's no way to figure it out. But I was always troubled, and there was always a battle within myself.

Karen first diagnosed me in 1987, my second season with the 49ers. I wanted no part of that conversation, though, and her telling me that was the slow beginning to our end in terms of our marriage. I figured my behavior was because of all those headaches my rookie year.

I didn't want to hear about manic depression or being bipolar, whatever they were calling it then. So every time over the years that she brought up the bipolar stuff, I would shut her out more and more. I lumped her in with everyone else trying to attack me when she was just trying to help. No one understood what was going on with me. They just wanted to say that something was wrong with me. Well, I knew that. I wasn't dumb. Obviously I was different than my teammates and coaches. I had some issues.

Being bipolar is about extremes. I could be the fun-loving, happiest guy in the world, or I could be out of control, the most horrific person imaginable, pissing on people's cars. There was no in between, no balance like other people.

It wasn't until 2002 that I finally accepted the diagnosis for what it was. Yeah, okay, I was bipolar, and a lot of things from my past started to make sense. Still, that's not when my life turned around. There were more highs and lows to come. Once you accept being bipolar, there are incidents from back in the day where you have a better understanding of—I don't want to say the thought process—at least how the mind could work that way.

Before my second season in the league, I renegotiated my contract with the 49ers. It was nothing major, mid-six figures, I guess. But while I'm reading it, I see that they don't want me riding a motorcycle. For any rational 23-year-old who previously has never ridden a motorcycle, this certainly shouldn't be an issue, right? That's like you getting your first job out of college, and the accounting firm says you can't listen to loud music at your desk. You're like, no problem, where's my first check?

That's not how my mind worked, though. For me this meant the team was telling me I couldn't do something. They were trying to keep me in a box. No one was going to tell me what I could or could not do. So I sign the contract, and guess what happens next? Yep, I bought a Harley-Davidson Sturgis and I jumped on it and rode it back to the team headquarters. I was a rebel.

I was an idiot.

Nobody told me anything about how to drive it and how you should never drive down the exact middle of the road because that's where the oil is from cars leaking. I hit the brakes in the middle of the road, and, of course, the motorcycle slid out from under me. The car behind me had to swerve to avoid hitting my dumb ass. I put a little scratch on the bike, but I was okay. I wasn't hurt. I just had a few scratches and bruises.

The 49ers find out and drag me in. They're all upset, saying that there was a clause in my new contract stating I can't do anything that's hazardous, like riding a motorcycle. They have the contract right there on the table, the one I just read a week or so earlier, but I played dumb.

I said, "Sorry guys, I'm a little slow and I read a little slow. I must have missed that."

Then I nicely explained to them that this little rule of theirs wasn't going to apply to me. I might not read quickly, but I understand real, real fast that no one is telling me how to or how not to live my life. You can tell me what to do on the football field; that's the deal. That's why I am paid, but off the field, that's my world.

As I was leaving the room, I turned around and said, "My goal is to become more efficient on riding my motorcycle." I don't think they knew what that meant. Hell, I'm not even sure what I meant. I just remember saying it and walking out. Maybe I was letting them know in my own way, that look, I'll try being careful on the bike, but I'm not selling it because you guys told me to. Again, what's ridiculous about all of this is not only had I never driven a bike, but I also had zero intentions of ever riding a motorcycle until seeing the wording in the contract. My mind just worked differently.

It's honestly a miracle I'm still here. Never mind writing a book, I'm talking about still breathing. That motorcycle was not a good idea. The several Harley-Davidson bikes thereafter were also not the best of ideas. If there is any advice I could give to someone who is bipolar or manic, it would be to get help, take your meds, and right after that, don't ride motorcycles—ever.

When you are going through those highs, those manic highs where you feel no pain, having a powerful motorcycle underneath you kind of gives you that feeling of flying. Throw in a few drinks, and again, I shouldn't be here.

My first season in Dallas, before Karen moved here with the kids, I was unsupervised and going out more than I usually would. I was out on my Harley and drinking at the Cowboys Sports Café one night during the week and I had a few more than I should have. When I drove home, I made a left turn and there I went, bike and all, across the street and down an embankment. I have no idea how I stayed on the bike, how the bike didn't fly out from under me. It scared the living daylights out of me, though. Holy God, I was driving faster than I should have been, too. That could have been lights out for me.

This is how my mind worked back then. I always drove my bike when I was going to be drinking because I stupidly figured how can you get a DUI riding a motorcycle? You're supposed to be swerving, going side to side, avoiding the middle, so that was my way of thinking ahead. Also, I didn't want to kill anyone. I'd kill myself, I was willing to take that risk, but I didn't want anyone else to die. I was riding a motorcycle instead of driving a big-ass truck and I figured most deaths in accidents are just the guy driving the bike. I was stupid beyond stupid. And driving home that night was maybe the dumbest thing I have ever done in my life. And that's really saying something, trust me.

At this point, which would have been in 1992, you'd figure the lightbulb would have come on when it came to me and bikes. Nope, I kept riding. I was a badass, and badasses rode bikes, at least that was my thinking. There were a few occasions when I drove my bike right into a bar or club, right through the front door, and in my delusional mind, I was a badass. In reality, I was just an ass, a jackass.

After a few of my back surgeries and recommendations from every doctor who ever looked at me, surely I was ready to stop riding my motorcycles. Of course not, I was a stubborn spoiled brat who couldn't think clearly. I went for a ride a few months after my fusion surgery in 1995, and those Harleys have some crazy vibration. There's no way to explain it if you haven't been on one. I came home, and my neighbor is out there mowing the lawn, and he starts walking over to say hi. I took one leg off with the bike still running and ended up falling face first into the ground. My legs and everything went numb, and I couldn't pick the bike up. My kids came running out of the house, and they are helping me, my neighbor is helping me. It was pathetic. My kids were crying, their father is bleeding and all scratched up, Karen was yelling at me, and I was in pain, too. That really hurt. Finally, this ended my days of riding a motorcycle. That's the last time I've been on one.

There are different levels of bipolar, and my case is extreme manic. That means my peaks and valleys are going to be the highest of highs and the lowest of lows. When you feel great, you start 100 projects and never finish any of them. You spend money, you buy 14 pairs of shoes, even though you end up wearing the same two pair all of the time. You go, go, go, and go some more. Those days at James Madison, or with the 49ers before my body started to fall apart, I would run and run like those Kenyan dudes. I would run sprints for hours. That's not normal. The only other players I ever saw run as much as I did were Jerry Rice and Michael Irvin, two Hall of Fame wide receivers. Those were peak days. Those were the days when I felt like Superman.

But you do so many things that you burn yourself out. Then guess what? What goes up, must come down. And that's a vicious bitch. When depression hits, it doesn't hit gradually. You go all the way down to the bottom fast, and that's when you want to lock yourself up in a room. That's when you don't want to talk to anybody. That's when you explode and become angry. That's when I did a lot of that crazy stuff that I don't really remember.

And I hated it so much. That bottom, that depression, it's like a fog, a cloud that covers your eyes. You look out the window, and all you see is the dirt. It doesn't matter if you are looking at the greenest farm in this country. All you see is dirt and misery. I don't wish that upon anyone, not even for a second of their lives. It's like someone has sucked out everything from your innermost soul that allows you to enjoy life.

And while some of the highs and lows can last for quite some time—weeks, even months, especially with the depression—it can be back and forth within a few hours as well.

Take a typical weekday during the football season, any of my seasons really. This wasn't every day. I'm just saying there were plenty like it. I would be there early, watching film by myself, focused on who knows what. There was no specific plan, whichever direction my mind was racing that day. I could spend two hours watching the wide receivers run patterns. Now, I was lined up across from a wideout zero times in my career, but still, I could tell you what routes they would be running based on the situation, the motion, the way they took their first step. I would grab some water and head into the locker room, laughing and joking around with everyone. Maybe I'd play cards or dominos. Then, without notice I would feel subdued and I would go sit at my locker alone for 20 minutes. I bet a lot of those nasty stories about me occurred in that time, when I just needed to be by myself, and someone tried talking to me. It's not their fault. They didn't know what was going on inside of me moment to moment. Hell, I didn't.

We next go out to practice, and I'm raging, I'm trying to kill someone. There's a story about me hitting Steve Young one time when he was wearing the red jersey at practice, which means he shouldn't have been hit. But I'm telling you in the moment I didn't see anything but a man who I was supposed to destroy. I'm not thinking about what jersey he's wearing. After practice I could transform back into nice Charles or crazy-ass Chuck. It just depended on the day.

Want to hear an interesting theory I've developed over the years, just piecing stuff together? Don't worry, it's not some conspiracy about landing on the moon or JFK. But I think Bill Walsh and the 49ers medical staff diagnosed me as bipolar during my rookie season, and they were medicating me. I was pretty well behaved with Bill there, but as much as I admired and respected him, it's not like I could have controlled the impulses on those bad days. Remember, they had all of us rookies visit with psychologists. And no one would have done more research on something like that than Bill. Maybe Karen talked with him, I don't know. I never asked anyone and still haven't to this day.

What I do know is that the 49ers were always giving me a lot of medicine. Not pain meds, not supplements. They would give me pills and say it was for inflammation. But I asked around, and no one else was taking any pills for inflammation. And then they would change it up here and there, saying, "Take this. It will help with the headaches." They would say all kinds of stuff. Looking back, I should have known something was up. But I was a football player. You take what they give you and stay focused on your task.

Sometimes I'd be feeling great, feeling normal, and that scared me, so I would stop taking the meds, which is ridiculous to think about. I just wasn't used to that. And they would come and find me, saying, "Charles, you need to take this. Here, take this." And sometimes I would, and sometimes I wouldn't. My best guess is that they diagnosed me from the beginning because it doesn't take much to figure out that there's a problem when a guy is off the wall for two or three weeks and then doesn't talk to anyone for a month. Sadly, for me, I didn't understand the difference between who I was on and off the meds. I was a mess.

My mind-set was that my silence would ignite my violence, and trust me, you didn't want me to go silent. I was so crazy, just so much crazy. Thank the Good Lord I somehow came through. I saw Bill Walsh talking about me in a television interview once, and he said I was a manic depressant. This was when I was playing, so Bill definitely knew. He never brought it up to me probably because he knew I would be angry with him for saying so, just like I was angry with Karen when she mentioned it.

Again, no one said they were giving me meds for the depression, just that I should keep taking them. Even during the offseason, they would give me a bottle and say, "Keep taking these. These will make you feel better."

I knew I was different. As a child, in college, and then in the NFL, there wasn't a day I woke up thinking I was like everyone else. There was something off. Those of us who are bipolar, we know we're acting differently. We just can't control it. Now that I realize what I have, I know I do not have a chance in life unless I take my medicine. What the medicine does is it allows me time to think about what I'm going to do instead of just reacting. I was always in a reactionary mode. Now I'm able to think a little bit clearer. From that standpoint for the first time in my life, I have freedom. I can be me—at least the balanced me.

The medicine gives me that opportunity to listen to the actual words someone is saying, to have a filter, rather than just me making the leap that I am being attacked and reacting. That was my deal. My top would blow really quickly, too. Back in the day, I might have been giving a speech and I'd say a joke, but I'd see someone over there laughing and then I'd forget about the speech because I'd think they were laughing at me, even though I had just said something funny. Yeah, my mind worked much differently than most.

I consciously use different techniques now that I have learned from doctors, clinics, whatnot, and they allow me to stay calm and focused. Ninety seconds. At 90 seconds everything will pass, so you just have to take a deep breath for 90 seconds and you will diffuse yourself. It's all kinds of little things they taught me like that.

There are a lot of misconceptions about mental illness and knowing right from wrong. I talk to young men and woman about mental illness all the time. I travel the country and something I see often is whenever someone does something wrong, something bad, the immediate reaction is, oh, they have a mental illness. And yes, they weren't in control when they acted like they did, but that isn't the same thing as not knowing right from wrong.

I have a mental illness, but guess what? I know right from wrong.

My mother raised me in the church, and after the fact, after I came out of the fog, I'd be like, wow, what have I done?

So it's not like we're blind to our actions. We deal with the guilt, the repercussions of our actions. There have been many times when the guilt has consumed me to the point that I've thought about killing myself. Many, many times.

While we are talking about misconceptions, there has been some speculation, some people saying, "Okay, if he wasn't bipolar, if he wasn't crazy, would Charles Haley have been as good of a football player as he was?" I think that's BS. If people think that, that's fine. That's their opinion. But trust me, I would have loved the chance to play my NFL career again while taking the proper medications. I think I would have done just fine and probably left the league with a few more friends, too.

Yeah, when I was up, that helped me work my ass off, but being down was tough because when the majority of severe bipolar people are depressed, they can't get out of bed. I know because that happened to me after my playing career. It was the love of football, the love of the game, and not wanting to let down my teammates that got me out of bed. I busted my ass at work because my father worked two and three jobs so I could eat and have this chance. Do people really think on the days I was down that I was staying home during the season? Hell no. I was there every day, busting my ass any way I could. That love was able to overcome the manic depression.

And it helped me as a father, too, because I would come home, and the negative energy was worn out. By the time my family joined me in Dallas for my second season with the Cowboys in 1993, we instituted a 30-minute rule for when I walked into the house. At that point I wasn't ready to be Dad just yet. I needed to decompress, so I went to my room and just lay there for 30 minutes. Then I'd come out and play with the kids, have dinner, and talk with Karen.

That sensitive, emotional side was a side of me that I never let people see. I always let people see the angry, out-of-control Chuck. Only my family, my kids, knew the real Charles then. My home life during those years was actually pretty fantastic. It was really great. They are some of the happiest memories of my life. Karen was in control of the house. She really controlled everything, and I was okay with that because I felt like she excelled at all the stuff I didn't, mostly communication. She was great with people, she did a great job with the finances, and she was a fantastic mother. And I had football. That was my outlet, which made it easier for me to stay in control at home.

My drinking was mostly under control during my playing career, too. During the season I drank on Sunday after the game, more so if we were on the road as I would drink on the plane. And then Monday night was our big drinking night. But then I was done for the week. Karen and I would go out on Thursdays, which was our date night. I had a routine, and routine is important with mental illness. That was probably the biggest problem after I stopped playing football. There was no routine.

I tried being a good husband and father, I really did. That was important to me. Still, I know I wasn't a good husband and I probably wasn't the greatest father, especially during my lows. I tried, though, and I continue to try every day. I was extremely fortunate to have Karen back then. I thank God for that. It didn't matter about my mental illness or my stubbornness to accept what I had. She wasn't going to back down. She stayed in my face. She kept me in control—at least as much as anyone could have. She didn't cut me any slack. I came home late one Monday, later than I was supposed to, and I went into the bedroom to sleep. She was like, "Oh no, you're not staying in here."

I said, "I own this house. I'm going to sleep right here."

She said, "Okay, okay, no problem."

She gets up and leaves the bedroom, and I'm just about asleep when I felt the coldest water I have ever felt thrown on me. She went and filled a bucket up with ice water. I jumped up—hell, that was the quickest first step of my career right there—and I headed to the guest bedroom upstairs. From that point on, when I came home late, it was the guest bedroom for me. I don't know what I was thinking messing around with her.

There has definitely been an evolution in my outlook toward violence. I'm a cupcake nowadays. I don't believe in violence of any kind. When I was first coming into the league, those first few years with the 49ers, I probably had a Malcolm X-type mind-set—doing things by any means necessary. Then I started having kids and reading more, and I became a hardcore, devout follower of Martin Luther King Jr.'s nonviolent ways. Of course, I believed in controlled violence in sports. I loved playing football, and the checks were pretty good, too.

The key for me was not exploding, just not losing my mind when I was on the field because after that burst it takes all of your energy away. I had to learn how to take that raw anger and channel it the correct way, harvest all of my energy, and focus in this tunnel so I could use a little bit here, a little bit there.

I couldn't allow myself to become mad about what my opponents were doing. Maybe they tried trash-talking me. Word got around the league quickly, and everyone was aware of my reputation, so I had to focus on my game and not allow anyone to work me into a rage. There were a lot of cheap hits, dirty hits, but the goal of that was simple: they wanted me to explode. They wanted me to fight back and focus on them, focus on revenge, rather than winning the game. But even with my mental illness, I was able to stay in control on the field and help my teammates. I never allowed an opponent to get in my head. Hell, I couldn't even get in my own head, so that probably helped.

So because of football, Karen, having kids, etc., my highs and lows were for the most part under control during my playing career. Obviously there are a lot of stories out there about me from that time, and

I'm not saying I was normal or didn't have issues. I'm just saying the bipolar was under control in comparison to how it spiraled downward after I retired for good in 1999.

There isn't just a single moment when you implode. There are several smaller episodes, and those just cause you to spiral more and more. And then one day you wake up and there you are at rock bottom. I was becoming more and more depressed, drinking a lot more than ever before and always talking about how worthless I was without football. What else did I have to offer society? I would talk about killing myself all the time, scaring Karen, my mother, my kids. It was a nightmare situation.

For the first time in my life, I had no outlet because football was finished. And my body was beat to hell. All the things I loved to do— playing football, running, riding my bike, playing with my kids, playing some basketball—I couldn't do any of it. This was during my late 30s, too, and then my early 40s. I wasn't an old man by any stretch of the imagination. My body was old, though.

Here's a life lesson: be a good listener and take action. I knew I had issues, but I was afraid to ask for help. I knew there was this five-year-old child inside of me screaming for help. I knew I hadn't received the help I needed because I was all messed up. That kid dominated my life because he kept screaming, and I punished other people for his pain. I wouldn't deal with it.

It was horrible. I felt like my own kids never understood me when they were younger, and that hurt. They'd see my explosions and then they would see me sit there and watch cartoons for hours. I don't know what that does to a kid. It couldn't have been easy for them. On my best days, I was Dr. Jekyll and Mr. Hyde. On my worst days, I was a scary, scary man.

I would sit in a room and just think of ways to kill myself. I wanted to die so many times—even with four beautiful and bright children, even with all of this money and a loving, caring wife. That's when you know it's bad. When you have it all and all you want to do is leave the world, that's the darkest of all those dark places. Somewhere in there, somewhere within the darkness, I made a conscious decision that I needed help. That process started in 2002, when I first accepted the diagnosis of being bipolar, which was a big step. My hell on earth was just heating up, though. This was no overnight success story.

The first problem was the initial medicine I was prescribed, which was Depakote. It did two things: it helped me sleep, and I gained a ton of weight. Within the first six months of taking it, I went from 245 pounds to 320. Yes, 320. I was huge. I just gained so much weight. Like every day, every hour. But I kept taking the medicine because I wanted to get better, I wanted to be normal, I wanted to be stable. I kept telling the doctor, "Hey, this weight gain isn't normal," and she said, "No, no, that's just one of the side effects." I said, "Okay, doc, but I'm going to be like 500 pounds here pretty soon, and that could be a problem."

It also made me so drowsy that I didn't want to even get out of bed. That was the toughest part. And after a while, I didn't feel like the doctor was listening to me or valuing my feedback, so I stopped taking it. The doctor couldn't fathom the physical pain I was in. I wanted to lose the weight. Having more weight to carry around was killing my back and knees, which already were painful as hell.

I was again a complete mess. The pain took over. With or without the medication, the pain dominated my life. I was irritated and mad, like, really mad. Here I am trying to do what the world wants me to, but I've gained all of this weight, and my body is in constant pain. And for the most part, I turned to alcohol, and yeah, there were some drugs. I did some non-prescribed drugs during that time. I just wanted to numb the pain.

So I had to find a doctor who could somehow help me deal with the bipolar, the pain, and my addiction. They kept trying to explain to me, stubborn-ass me, that the alcohol, the other drugs, all that crap I was doing was affecting the bipolar medicine. I couldn't grasp that—at least not then.

I went to rehab a couple of times for alcoholism. Of course, by then I could open up my own clinic and talk about alcoholism, the effects on the brain, how it stimulates the brain. Still, it didn't help me. I understood it all, but it didn't help me. I needed a dual diagnosis center and I finally found one, the La Paloma Treatment Center in Memphis, Tennessee, that worked, that helped me. This was 2011, and then I went again in 2012. The guy who ran the place is a recovering alcoholic, and he was also bipolar. This guy was just like me. Everybody from the janitor to the therapists and the counselors, even the guys that just check you into your room, everybody there had either some kind of addiction or mental illness. That's when the light turned on for me. I saw myself in a lot of those people and then I was able to see how different people acted when they came in.

I could see how the new medicine they put me on was changing my thought patterns, how I perceived situations, how I was seeing everybody else around me. It was all changing. My problem was always that I remembered, I obsessed really, about all the negative stuff people did or said to me, but I never remembered all the good stuff, all the positive words. My mind blocked those out.

My favorite aspect of being there at that recovery center was that for the first time in my life, I was able to have a conversation with someone and take it all in. The medicine was allowing me to hear the good and the bad and process both accordingly. As I've mentioned, I would talk with someone for 20 minutes and come away with a single word that I felt was negative and directed at me. Then I would translate that into that person hating me or talking bad about me, and that would become my reality, which of course was nothing close to being the actual reality. In the past I would take the medication, but then I would just stop for various reasons, and the alcoholism would take over. Thankfully, someone recommended that place in Tennessee. That was a life-changing experience.

I am always telling people around the NFL that some players who are struggling need this kind of place that deals with both mental illness and substance abuse. It doesn't make sense to deal with one or the other because they go together. The mental illness fueled my addictions of alcohol, drugs, whatever. Once I took control of the mental illness, the bipolar part, I didn't want to drink or take drugs. As I'm writing this, I haven't had a drink in four years now. I've had no drugs either, outside of my medication.

I'll be around people at a function or something, and if they offer me a drink, I'll be like, no thank you. It never crosses my mind to pick up a glass now. The issue was I never knew what was driving my need to drink. Now I understand it was the mental illness, the bipolar disorder. Perhaps the biggest impact the dual diagnosis center had on me came when they did some psychotherapy where we role-played. Other people played those in my life who hurt me, and I was able to talk with them, tell them the pain that they caused me.

We had to do that twice because the first time wasn't too successful. I became so angry that I slammed the chair I was sitting in. The doctor there was able to calm me down and he recommended that we not try it anymore, but the man who ran the place said, "Let's do it again." And it couldn't have been more successful the second time. We were peeling that onion off layer by layer and revealing my innermost feelings. Those had been locked up for a long time.

I started writing letters to people, to those who had made me angry and those who I treated poorly. I told them I regretted my actions. I let go of everything. It all came out. And you know what? I don't hate anymore. There is no one in this world I hate. I look at people for who they are. I'm not saying there's no anger inside of me. I still harbor a lot of anger for how some people in Gladys treated me, how some teachers and coaches treated my brothers and me at my high school. They did us no favors in getting us out of there. They never let us know there even was a way out.

I'm good now, though. My life is in a good place, and the best thing about it is I've directed other people to dual diagnosis centers. I've directed other people to my therapist here in Dallas, who is a dual diagnosis specialist, and there have been results. Nothing could please me more.

I'll go into an NFL locker room, start talking to guys, and they stand out. Guys are not looking you in the face. They want to look down at their feet. They're hiding. They're hiding the shame, the hurt, the pain. I know because I've been there. I tell these guys, not only Cowboys players, though I spend a lot more time at their training facility than with other teams, I tell them, "I'm committed to helping you out, but you have to be committed to me." I'm hands-on. I can teach them football stuff, but I can also teach them life skills. I can teach them about the consequences. I lost everything, I lost my family, I lost a lot of friends.

My kids didn't want to be around an angry ass, somebody who was going to blow up. They didn't want to go to dinner with me because they might say something completely innocent, and I'd blow up. It just ruined everybody's mood. During those dark days, when I was stressed, when I was in pain, I would erupt with anger. And when I get angry, I usually get really quiet. My kids knew all the signs. They knew when I was in a bad place.

The worst part about the whole deal was on Father's Day or my birthday. They would come to my house, hand me a gift or card, and then leave. I wouldn't see them again until who knows when because they didn't want to be around that Chuck, that angry asshole of a person.

Now I tell my kids all the time, "You have a right to be mad at me for my actions. You have every right in the world."

It's getting better, though. My son has been living with me for the last year or so, and I talk with all of my kids. I tell them, "Look, I am not angry with you for however our relationship is going to be. I love you all. I love you all unconditionally." I'll be paying every day of my life for how stupid I was, the hurt I brought.

The only downside for them, and I kid them about this, is that when I was screwing up I would try to cheer them up by buying them something. Now that I'm not screwing up anymore, I'm not buying them anything else.

I'm always here for them, though. They know the deal. If they want to be mad at me for the past, then that's fine. I respect that. If they want me to be their father, I'm here. I'm always here for them. And again, it has been a lot better of late, and I couldn't be happier. C.J., my son, he was always there for me. When I was at my lowest, when the depression wouldn't allow me to get out of bed for weeks at a time, he would drive over and bring me food. He would sit on the bed and try to get me to eat. He would try, beg me really, to stand up and take a walk with him even around the house. This was when he was in high school and college. I didn't even attend his college graduation. I was so depressed, so out of it, I missed it and didn't really even think about it.

People hear that and assume I'm a horrible person. It's so difficult to understand. You don't have reality. It is just not there. All you think about is yourself, and I thought I was worthless. I didn't believe I was worthy of my family's love. I always felt like everybody was against me, even my kids. That's how depression and mental illness work.

I tell people all the time that I spent 35 years locked up in a closet emotionally, but I will not spend one more day not having fun, not expressing my feelings or my love. I don't live on the other side of that emotional track anymore. I don't let people steal my joy. I'm not being controlled any longer by my illness or addiction.

I'm no longer a reactionary person. I'm no longer a person who wants to attack. I'm no longer that person who has to think, *oh no, what did I just do?* I allowed people, most of them undeservingly, to bring out my anger and my violence. That person doesn't exist anymore.

R.I.P. Chuck.

Now I make choices with my emotions. I can stop and think about how I should deal with this. I try and listen to every word someone says. I even ask them what they meant by something. I'm not perfect, but I'm a whole lot better. Another big change is that process inside of my head that was always obsessed with getting even. Everything was driven by revenge. If someone pissed me off, I needed to piss them off and more so. That was the basis for a lot of my issues with teammates and coaches.

At the end of the day now, when I close my eyes, I close that day off. I don't worry about yesterday or even tomorrow. I just worry about today. Today is big for me. And every day that I'm able to live my life in that manner, that's a good day. That's why every day is so important to me. I'm a goals guy. In my bathroom, right where I brush my teeth, it's on the wall. It says, "Who Am I?" And then on the back of the door, it says, "How Do You Want to Be Remembered?" And the way I live life is simple: what I do today will affect how I will be remembered. That's my mantra right now when I'm talking to those with the kinds of problems I had. My goal is to be a better man each day, to look people in the eye and say, "Hey, this is what I did, this is what it took for me to change, and maybe you should try that. Let me help you."

I believe God is giving me a mission to talk with football players, with anyone really, about mental illness. At the end of the day, you need to hear firsthand what someone has been through. I've been in those places where death looks more appealing than living and I've survived. Let me help you. It's so frustrating to hear everyone talking about how it's beyond reason that some kid making $9 million can't stop using drugs. It's not that he's a drug addict. It's that he can't deal with his world. It's mental illness. Then they suspend him and take away football, which is basically putting him in prison.

There's no movement on this. NFL commissioner Roger Goodell and executive vice president of football operations Troy Vincent do a good job with a lot of issues, but there's no movement on mental illness. A guy comes back from a suspension, and he's labeled a drug addict. That's not usally the issue. Help the players get the help they need. They have an 800 number to call if a guy wants to kill himself. Come on, a guy has reached the point of committing suicide, and he's going to stop and call the 800 number? *Hi, how are you doing? How's the family? Yeah, so I don't know you, but I decided to call a complete stranger and, oh, by the way, I'm going to kill myself. Can you help?*

The league is not proactive. They put psychiatrists in the locker room, but they don't realize that the players think those counselors are company people, which means they don't ask for help. So what good are they? The NFL needs to have independent people, former players, in the locker rooms every week. The players have to know that they can trust who they are talking to.

Most players think that if their teams find out they have a mental illness, then the team has a bargaining chip against them, so they'd rather not seek help because they want to stay in power. People fear what they don't understand instead of trying to understand what they fear. I know what I've been through, I know the way that I used to think, I know the way I used to behave, and I see that. I know who I was, and if I see that in someone else, I'm going to stop and try to make a difference.

I tell people all the time, I tell my kids, I tell players, guys with mental illness, that I did A, B, C, and D, and you know what? People can judge me for that. They can, that's their right. But remember Matthew 18:21-22: "Then came Peter to him, and said, Lord, how oft shall my brother sin against me, and I forgive him? Till seven times? Jesus saith unto him, I say not unto thee, Until seven times, but Until seventy times seven." So I ask people to forgive me because I regret these things. Whatever we need to do so we can move past my sins, let's try to do that.

I go to counseling all the time. I'm honest now with both myself and those who are trying to help me. I used to go to counseling and I would read up about what we were going to talk about and then go in there and argue with the person who was trying to help me. Now I go in, and we talk about what I'm feeling. And I try to be that counselor for a lot of guys who are struggling like I was. I'm on my own dime, too. If a guy calls me in Arizona and says he needs my help, I'm flying there. That's how much I want to help.

I'm trying. I really am. I want to help. I want to be a better person. Am I perfect? No, not by a long shot. A current NFL player called me not long ago and asked me to fly out. I was there the next day, and the guy says, "I don't have any problem. I decided I'm okay." I was so pissed off that I hit him in the balls. I'm not getting any brownie points for that one, but it sure made me feel good.

Still, there is no one who has been through what I've gone through, the pain, the suffering, and the rebirth. I know the path out of this misery and I'll go with you to wherever that path leads us. Salvation lies within.

Chapter 12

Hall of Fame Induction

I WASN'T THE KIND of guy to ever worry about the future. I never thought about playing college football in high school. I didn't even know that was a possibility, didn't know anything about scholarships. I was oblivious to everything outside of my hometown. Then at James Madison, the last thing on my mind was playing in the NFL. As I said, the first NFL game I ever attended or watched was the first one I played in. That's the God's honest truth. So, it's not going to surprise anyone that the Pro Football Hall of Fame wasn't an objective of mine during my playing career. I hadn't even heard of it until we played in the Hall of Fame game in 1987. I couldn't tell you anything about the game—or really any other preseason game for that matter—but I remember my childhood hero, "Mean" Joe Greene, was being inducted. That was really cool.

The day after his induction, I saw Greene on the field during the coin toss. It was amazing to meet him and be a small part of a weekend of football history. My mind-set during my playing career was about winning. Each week the goal was winning that game, winning championships. I don't believe athletes are thinking about the Hall of Fame or having their number retired by the teams they play for. I knew I was a pretty good player. I was named to some Pro Bowls and All-Pro teams, but I was never into that stuff. And I didn't really know what the standard was for something like the Hall of Fame. I still don't. If winning was taken into account, my teams won 77 percent of their games, including the playoffs. Only Tom Brady has a higher winning percentage among those who played 100 games in the Super Bowl era. Since sacks became an official statistic in 1982, no one has more than my four in the Super Bowl. And I'm still tied for fifth all-time in postseason sacks with 11.

Initially, I wasn't that concerned with whether I made the Hall of Fame. Players become eligible for induction five years after they retire, so I was first eligible in 2004. But for 11 years, every time I left the house, it seemed like someone was asking me about why I wasn't in the Hall of Fame. I never really knew what the answer was. A lot of folks said it was because of my relationship with the media, which is in charge of the voting process. I wasn't exactly warm and friendly with them. Actually, I was a world-class jerk for the most part. I tried not to think about it, but it was tough when everyone was always asking.

Shortly after they opened the George W. Bush Presidential Library in Dallas, I was invited to a function there. So I show up with Karen and my four kids, and the woman at the entrance table tells me that I'm the only one on the list. She was very polite and said she was sorry, but that there wasn't anything they could do. I said, "Ma'am, I don't deal with problems, I deal with solutions, so you need to find a damn solution to your problem because my family is attending with me."

She stood up and walked away, which to me meant that I could take my family in. My family didn't think so. Karen and the kids are all scared and nervous, but I'm like, screw it, let's go. We walk in, find seats, and within a few minutes, I'm talking to former secretary of state Condoleezza Rice. She was really nice. Then we hear them announce President George W. Bush and First Lady Laura Bush, and they walk in.

I've met presidents before at the White House after winning a few of our Super Bowls. I met Bill Clinton twice. He was cool, always smiling, laughing. I liked him a lot. And I met old man Bush. He was a little more formal, but that was my first time at the White House, so I was kind of in awe of it all. I'm guessing not a lot of kids from Gladys have been inside the White House.

Kind of spur of the moment, I decide to walk over and introduce myself to President G. W. Bush. And as I'm walking over, these Secret Service guys come to his side like I'm a threat or something. I said,

"Mr. President, you may as well tell them to rest because I'm going to get me a damn hug." And he starts laughing and says, "Well, come on then, 'Big Haley,'" and he wraps his arms around me and squeezes me tight. This was a world-class hug. In fact it wasn't so much a hug as he jumped into my arms.

Bush had launched himself into me with such vigor and was squeezing me so hard that I thought the Secret Service was going to have to separate us and probably bury my ass in concrete. Now, keep in mind that you never fully recover from four-level back fusion surgery, and the only thing I'm thinking is that when people are driving up to the library that next morning they'll see the construction workers pouring out the concrete, under which I'm going to be another Jimmy Hoffa. I mean, it took everything in me not to break that hug. That man is strong. After that, I asked him if he could take a photo with me and my family, and he said, "Yes, absolutely Big Haley. I have to run over there for a minute, but I'll come back."

I go sit down with my family, and about five minutes passes, and let me tell you, that room became old and white in a hurry. All of these important people are walking in, and I'm thinking that this photo isn't happening. I even told my kids, I said, "You know what? We aren't going to get that photo after all." I didn't even see him. It looked like he had left.

About 30 seconds after I told them that, I hear from across the room, "Hey, Big Haley, where are you?" And it was President Bush. He said, "You're next. Bring your family over here." I stood up and said, "Yes, sir, I may be a goddamn Democrat, but this guy is all right."

And Karen kicked the heck out of me. I can feel it now. She kicked me on my ankle. It was worse than any hit on the football field. And I start jumping around in pain, and everyone in that place is staring at me like, oh, my God, he's crazier than hell. You should have seen the looks on those faces.

He came through, though. We went over and took a photo with him, and guess what? Even he asked me, "When are they going to put you in the Hall of Fame?" I just smiled. Everyone kept asking, former teammates, family, friends—the president. I went to Starbucks one time, and the guy at the register wanted to know. I didn't have any answers.

As for what I was doing—outside of my depression and substance abuse issues—for those 15 years between playing and entering Canton, there was a little of this and a little of that. My former teammate with the 49ers, Matt Millen, called me about being an assistant coach when he was named general manager of the Detroit Lions in 2001.

That sounded pretty good to me, especially the part about being able to stay around the game. Matt and I talked football for hours when we were teammates, and he knew how much I loved watching film. He's a good guy, I love him very much, and he was a heck of a linebacker back in the day. I really wished it had worked out better for him with that gig. He's one of my favorite people in this world. My coaching career, at least as far as an official title, lasted two years. And we stunk. We finished 2–14 and 3–13. We lost 27 games in two years. During my first seven years in the league, my teams lost fewer regular-season games than that.

I don't do losing well, though admittedly there were other issues with the full-time coaching thing. It was just so time consuming, but it's one thing to put all of that time and effort into a purpose and succeed. Then there's putting in 16-hour days and losing every week. That was not rewarding for me. For me to kill myself, be it playing or coaching, there needs to be that success.

Then you have guys who don't want to listen. They were more than content to continue doing the same thing they were doing rather than changing their technique, their attitude, their film study, their dedication, and maybe having some success. I mean, maybe say, "Hey, you know what, this guy won five Super Bowls. Maybe we should listen to what he's telling us." It wasn't just me either. It was any number of coaches. For those two years, the lack of listening, the lack of success, that took a big toll on me. I could have remained in coaching. There have been other offers, but I made a decision that I was going to find another way to make money and give back to the game.

I am always, until my last days in this world, going to be involved in football—just not as a full-time coach. I live in Dallas and go work with the Cowboys' defensive linemen all the time. If I'm in San Francisco or at a camp, I'll work with anyone who wants my help. High school players, college, I'll teach whoever wants to listen.

I spent a lot of time around soccer, the sport my daughters played. I trained a lot of athletes with a focus on being mentally strong. That's the key to any athletic endeavor, being mentally strong. I would say 99 percent of the time the body is strong and prepared for success, but it's the mental part of the game that destroys people. Know what I should mention here, just in regard to me coaching—or even me as a teammate—as a person? I think sometimes I'm too blunt, and that may turn guys off. I understand that more and more as I grow older. That doesn't mean I'm going to change, though. I don't sugarcoat anything. When I talk with football players—from NFL to Pop Warner—I tell them, "I'm not your momma, I'm not your God, I'm not your priest, and I'm not your wife." I'm not going to treat them with kindness or kid gloves. If they don't want to be a part of that, then move on. If they're okay with that, we move from there. If they stay out there on the field and work with me, they're going to work hard.

I want nothing from them. I'm not looking for money or kudos. I just want to help and give back to the game. If they learn my techniques on pass rushing, I guess I'll kind of live through them. And that keeps me feeling relevant. We all like to be relevant.

I can show them the water, but it's up to them to drink it. I stress to these guys again and again: they can achieve their dreams and beyond if they commit. It's about hard work and dedication. That's the key to success in any walk of life. That might sound simplistic, but it's the truth. Maybe you'll catch a break or two along the way in terms of opportunity like an assistant coach from James Madison, who was watching some film on me, or having a Bill Walsh as a coach. But ask those who have succeeded, and I'm telling you that nearly all are going to say it's hard work and dedication.

Anyhow after six years, I was named a finalist to the Hall of Fame in 2010. That means the voters would debate about whether or not I should be inducted. They vote the day before the Super Bowl every year at whichever city the game is being played. The finalists are put up at a hotel, and you wait. That first year, when the phone call came from the Hall of Fame saying I wasn't elected, I was upset. I was pretty pissed off. Now, that was because when it happened, at that particular time and place, I was really depressed. I was going through some dark days. And I think just being a finalist for the first time, that kind of temporarily revived me.

So then there was this huge letdown. I decided at that moment that, no matter what, I would attend the Super Bowl every year. Whether I was a finalist, was elected, was never elected, I was going to the Super Bowl. That way, regardless of the entire Hall of Fame stuff, I wouldn't get depressed. I was going for the game, not the vote.

During that first time I was not inducted, I really threw a fit. I locked everybody out of the room, even my kids. I wouldn't come out. They had to get another room. So going forward, the plan was to go to the Super Bowl. That way I would never put my family through another nightmare like that. And the plan worked out. I was good after that.

Everything changes after you are a finalist for the first time. All the emotions change. I was honestly surprised to be selected as a finalist, but then going forward, I would have been disappointed if I wasn't a finalist because then you are going backward. I'm all about moving forward in life, not backward. First, I wanted out of Gladys and then I wanted a great life coming out of James Madison, whether it was with football or not. Then once you start winning, you never want to stop. It's always what's next, so after becoming a finalist, there was only one more next step.

I was a finalist again in 2011, then the year after that, and the year after that. Damn, that wasn't enjoyable, especially when everyone was telling me that this should be a slam-dunk.

Know what, though? God has truly blessed me. Those years were the best of my post-career. I was taking my meds and I wasn't drinking, so a lot was going great for me, which helped when that phone rang in my hotel room the day before each of those Super Bowls. When you don't make it, they call you. When you make it, there's a knock on your door.

On January 31, 2015, in Phoenix, there was finally a knock on my door. The president of the Hall of Fame, a man named David Baker, was there smiling. And before he could say a word, I said, "Damn, I'm in. *I'm in.*"

He said, "Welcome to the Pro Football Hall of Fame." And we shook hands.

That was one of the best days of my life. My legs became weak. I needed to go in the bathroom and cry. In terms of football, in terms of the profession I worked in, there's no higher honor, though being recognized by the teams you played for, that's pretty special, too.

The Cowboys inducted me into their Ring of Honor in 2011, and that was pretty spectacular, pretty humbling. That's the best of the best. Men like Bob Lilly, Roger Staubach, Tony Dorsett, and my team-mates—Michael Irvin, Emmitt Smith, Troy Aikman, and Larry Allen—are in there. Hell, Tom Landry is in there.

That was incredibly kind of Jerry Jones to do. Because I only spent five seasons with the Cowboys, it would have been understandable if they hadn't included me. But Jerry wanted to make a statement to the Hall of Fame voters on my behalf. That's such a classy touch. Jerry is always looking out for me. He made that promise to me the first time we spoke, that he would have my back, and he always has.

During the 2015 season, the Cowboys presented me with my Hall of Fame ring between the first and second quarters of a home game against the Seattle Seahawks. Jerry gave a little speech and then gave me the ring. It was great seeing him and his big-ass country smile. I tell him all the time, "That's a $4 billion smile right there," and he just laughs. I'm always talking trash to him. I said, "We don't see you out at practice anymore. You must not love the Cowboys anymore." He just shakes his head and laughs. Jerry is so cool because you think he's this big, powerful guy and he is, but he can take a joke as well as anyone. He's still one of the guys and he's such a great sport. Sometimes, I find myself wondering why he likes me, but he does, and I'm so fortunate. There is no one more loyal than Jerry.

In 2015 the 49ers inducted me into their Hall of Fame. That meant a lot because I didn't think they would recognize me with how my first stint there ended. They said some harsh things, and I definitely said some harsh things. Going back at the end of my career probably helped how it eventually played out. I'm not great at explaining myself when I'm being honored, but those two moments with the Cowboys and the 49ers were right there with anything in my life. And both fanbases have just always treated me so beautifully. I was a defensive player. We aren't the ones who usually receive the love and attention. It's the quarterbacks, it's the running backs, it's the receivers. But those fanbases have some of the best fans out there.

I was a shy farm boy, and to be honest, signing autographs always scared the hell out of me because I didn't want to misspell someone's name and have them make fun of me or think I was dumb. I worked hard at James Madison to graduate, but I'm still a little slow at reading and writing. So if there's some fan out there thinking I was a dick for not signing an autograph one time back in the day, I'm regretful.

The fans are everything. Without them there is no game. The fans are the reason why I was paid to play football. So I decided at some point—this was during my career, actually—that if I didn't want to be bothered by some fan, then I should stay in my house. That's the deal. I owe every single man or woman who ever bought a ticket or a jersey or watched a game on television. I owe them all. Football doesn't owe me a thing. I owe football and I owe the fans. If they want to talk football, take a picture, want an autograph, I'm going to do whatever they ask of me. When I hear about a player saying no, it just makes me cringe. We are forever indebted to the fans, and that's an honor for me.

I will say this: we, as in athletes, are people, too. We have our own lives and we have places to be. We have responsibilities. If I'm trying to coach my daughter's soccer game, I really don't want to sign autographs and take pictures in the middle of the second half. Wait until the game is over and I've talked to the team, and then I'm yours.

I went to the car wash one time on the way to a doctor's appointment and I'm there talking with everyone, signing for like 30 minutes and I have to go. I'm already late. I'm always late. And someone is pissed off because I have to leave. We're trying. The majority of us are honestly trying. It's just that we have kids and doctor's appointments, too, like anyone else.

Some mornings I hit Starbucks at, say 9:00 or so, and boom, I'm in there for two hours. And that's great. If I don't have anything going on that morning, I'll tell stories and hang out. I've also found that it's really healthy for me. It clears my head, and I'm not sitting around by myself battling with depression or whatever. I wouldn't quite say I've become a people person, but I enjoy it. My favorite part really is just talking football with folks. So many people love the game. It's really wonderful to see and be a part of.

August 8, 2015, was also wonderful. The Pro Football Hall of Fame induction took place on a picturesque Saturday evening. Running back Jerome "the Bus" Bettis; wide receiver Tim Brown; linebacker Junior Seau, who tragically committed suicide in 2012; guard Will Shields; center Mick Tingelhoff; and contributors Ron Wolf and Bill Polian were enshrined with me. I couldn't have been more proud to stand alongside those guys. I only wished Junior was there with us.

There are two responsibilities for those of us inducted. We need to select who will present us and we need to write a speech. Oh, and I had my teeth whitened a few times. I wanted to look good smiling on that stage. That all sounds pretty easy, right? Well, in theory, perhaps.

But I fought the Hall of Fame for months. We went back and forth, a bunch of phone calls. Yes, I know, everyone is thinking that only Charles could be inducted into the Pro Football Hall of Fame and find a problem. My issue, though, was that I wanted two presenters, one from the 49ers, Eddie DeBartolo, and one from the Cowboys, Jerry, of course. For my money they are the two best owners in the history of professional sports. And they said, "No, you have to pick one." I told them, "Look, times are changing, and the majority of players being inducted going forward are going to have played for multiple teams." They politely said, "Well, that might be true, but we're still going to force everyone to choose just one presenter. The ceremonies are going too long as it is. We can't find reasons to make it longer."

If Bill Walsh was still alive, the choice would have taken me two seconds. In fact, I told him that the last time we spoke. That if I was ever inducted, he would present me. He said, "Charles, I'm not going to be able to do that, but it would have been my honor."

That's how I ended up making my decision. I figured I owed it to Bill to have someone from the 49ers present me. That's no knock on Jerry or the Cowboys. I hate that some fans took it that way. I live in Dallas. I'm around the Cowboys every week of the season. And I love Jerry, and he knows that. In the end it was just about my relationship and admiration for Bill Walsh. And Mr. D has been wonderful to me as well.

This was one of those moments where I would have dealt with it much differently five years earlier. I was becoming more and more angry with the Hall of Fame for not allowing me to have two presenters. That other person almost came out. Chuck almost made what would have been an unfortunate appearance. Instead, I kept taking my medication and worked through it. A lot of people close to me, Jerry included, said not to push it and just enjoy my moment. So, I let it go.

Those few days in Canton, Ohio, will never be topped. That was the ultimate. All of my family and friends, the Hall of Fame members, people saying nice things to me and me actually appreciating the words rather than looking for something negative, the opportunity for me to share my story, it was all so inspirational for me. There were so many hugs, so many handshakes, it was magical. It was like going to the Football Disney World, the Magical Kingdom of Football and Family. I have never been that happy in my life.

My family was there: my ex-wife who I still love so much; my pride and joy, my four beautiful kids, Madison, C.J., Brianna, and Princess; my mother; and four brothers. My father wasn't able to make it. He's had both his legs amputated because of diabetes, but I was thinking about him back home in Gladys. The process was also hectic. The Hall does a great job of planning everything, but wow, I felt like a sheep that is being herded from one field to the other because there was no downtime. There weren't many opportunities to have a conversation for longer than a minute. It was organized chaos. I was able to hug my mother for about five minutes. That was the longest and most meaningful hug of my life. My momma was proud of me. That says it all, right?

I'm now looking forward to returning every year and being able to sit back and soak it all in while watching each incoming class and just being a small part of it. For me, a guy who doesn't really like the spotlight but enjoys being around those guys and football, that's going to be a lot of fun. Obviously, it's an honor of a lifetime, and you're thrilled beyond words, but that was a tiring-ass week.

A lot of these players whom I admire so much are getting old, and I want to at least have the chance to shake their hands and tell them how much I admire them and thank them for the sacrifices they made. Those players and coaches in the 1950s, 1960s, even the 1970s, they weren't banking millions of dollars. But they were laying the foundation, allowing the country to fall in love with football. They were creating a new pastime, and that allowed for all of those big-money television deals and guys like me to make a nice living. So that's what I'm excited about, having the chance to go back each summer and take advantage of the opportunity for new friendships to develop, hearing some of the stories from another time, and just enjoying myself.

As for the speech, standing up there being inducted into the Pro Football Hall of Fame was awkward for me because of my mental state being what it is. I'm always thinking people just build you up so they can tear you down. I know that's not the reality of it, but thoughts like that enter my mind. Not as much as they once did, but they still do.

I didn't write my speech word for word. I just made some notes, the thoughts and ideas I wanted to share. The only notes were just making sure I thanked the right people. Every other word I said came from my heart, which was all passion and love. I tend to talk better that way anyhow. The reading process tends to slow me down. There was a lot of positive feedback about my speech, and that was an honor. I think a lot of people were surprised by my words. Maybe they were expecting crazy Charles from my playing days when the media couldn't get more than two words out of me...and I'm guessing you know what two words those were.

For my speech I talked about how my life spiraled out of control with my manic depression. I talked about how I've grown since being diagnosed, how I have changed, how I now try to make a difference in the lives of younger players dealing with some of the issues I dealt with. I don't want them to feel alone like I often did. I spoke about the great owners and coaches of my career, my teammates who dealt with all of my BS, and all those behind the scenes who were friends when they didn't have to be, when I was hell on wheels. And I talked about how the one thing I learned from all of my teammates is to play unselfishly, that the team matters. We need to go back to that. It's not about individuals; it's about team. That's the only way we can have success. As a team and in life.

As for the finish to my speech, well, for me there was only one place to conclude. I said, "In closing I'd like to say one thing is I used to read two books of the Bible all the time. They were Psalms, because of King David, when he said, 'I walk through the valley of the shadow of death, I should fear no evil.' I always thought everybody was against me, so that was the first warrior in the Bible, too, so I used that. And then Job, conviction. Hey, he was a rock. He would not be moved, and that's the way I feel about football, guys. When I step out on that field, guys, I was determined to be the best every play, not some plays, but every play. Guys, thank you so much."

I think I spoke with the media more between being voted in and the actual Hall ceremony than during my whole career combined. Going forward, though, any time someone wants to talk, I'm all for it. I want to be an example for today's players and I tell these young men that my faults are my strengths now. I tell kids that my lack of education before James Madison caused me to work harder, to become knowledgeable enough to graduate.

In order to understand a person, you have to understand what he's been through and then what he's willing to do to sacrifice to succeed. God gave me the chance that so many young men from my world never have, and that's going to college. So at that point, I owed it to

God, my parents, and myself to bust my ass. I try and convey that message every time I speak with someone, be it the media or otherwise.

When I am speaking, I make sure to talk about my regrets. That's important. I can't get anyone to learn anything from me if I don't tell the truth. My favorite part of now being a member of the Pro Football Hall of Fame, the Cowboys Ring of Honor, and the 49ers Hall of Fame is that they can never take that away from me. No one is going to show up at my door one morning and say, "Charles, we're sorry to inform you that you are no longer a member. Here's your bust." Long after I'm gone, my bust is going to be in Canton. That's forever.

Chapter 13

Reflection

MY EX-WIFE KAREN will always have a special place in my heart. Ours is not one of those ugly divorces where we hate each other. We're still very cordial, very kind to each other. We've gone to Canada with the kids since separating, and she came to my Hall of Fame induction with the kids. I screwed that marriage up, but I still love her immensely. And I think she cares deeply for me.

We were married 19 years. The divorce took place in 2006. It's been a healing process because I kept doing stupid stuff after we split. That woman tried so hard. She gave me chance after chance after chance to mend the fence, and I just couldn't get my act together to make it happen. I have nothing bad to say about Karen.

The big, bad Charles from my playing days, that was just an image. I loved taking care of my family. And we had a lot of good times, especially during my career. The bad times were mostly after I retired. My family came first for me. To this day I tell Karen, "Hey, it wasn't until divorce do us part. It's until death do us part." I still treat her as if we were married. And we're still friends. I think that friendship will last forever. She knows all of my stories and she knows me. She knows my love and my pain.

Karen is mean, a lot like my mother. And she is demanding. She demanded respect and demanded that I do A, B, and C, and I'm glad she did. The Hall of Fame induction wouldn't have been the same if she wasn't there. She's been such a big part of my life. She helped me keep it together, at least as much as I could. I wouldn't be here without her, and my career wouldn't have been as successful. Our relationship worked out pretty well. I was the gatherer and I let her take care of everything else. After we bought a nice house, she furnished the entire thing. I didn't make a purchase and I was fine with that. Our person-alities balanced each other and allowed us to take advantage of our strengths.

The part that is still difficult is getting used to living alone. I have never lived alone. One of my kids, including Charles Jr., might stay with me for a stretch here or there, which is great. For the most part, though, it's just me. The loneliness comes from not being able to talk to an adult, go to dinner. I want a companion, not a bunch of dates and all that stuff. I don't date. I'm not in a hurry to run into anybody's arms. I'd just rather stay at home. I'm a homebody.

I have always loved kids—my kids, anyone's kids. I didn't neglect my fatherly duties when they were younger. I changed diapers, I burped them, I did all of that stuff. If the baby was crying after practice, I woke up and took care of her. We had our kids more or less every two years, so that helped, having them spread out like that.

Regardless, I loved being a father. I loved it from the first moment. I could come home in the worst pain imaginable, but if one of my kids wanted to play on the floor, have me take them to the playground, or teach them to ride a bike, I was there. It also helped that I was addicted to watching cartoons, so they would always join me. We would watch on Saturday mornings for hours. I was the big kid with my little kids. Life doesn't get any better than that.

My children have done really well for themselves. My three oldest have graduated college, Princess was a valedictorian in high school, Brianna was homecoming queen, and my youngest has signed to play soccer at Stanford. It's incredible how we can change our worlds in a single generation. I struggled to read and write growing up, and none of my brothers went to college. And now we have valedictorians and a kid at Stanford.

I have a great relationship with my kids. Now, I can be kind of hard. I'm not a grumpy old man, at least not yet, but I'm a little stuck in my ways. Like I tell them, "Your mother loves you unconditionally, but the moment you don't do what I want, that condition is gone from me." I'm kidding, of course, but I like to have fun with them. I'll say to them, "Daddy knows best," and they just roll their eyes.

The only thing that I regret about how I raised my kids is sending them to private schools. They never fully developed some common sense stuff. Or maybe it's more street smarts than common sense. They're book smart and they are all going to kick ass in this world. They have no limitations. They can do all this smart stuff on their computers and tablets, but they don't know how to write a check or mail an envelope—little things like that drive me absolutely crazy. But I realize it was different back in my day. They taught some life lessons back then.

My kids also have no problem letting me know how much more educated they are than me. I laugh most of the time—hell, I'm proud of what they have done—but once in a while I can't help myself and I'll say, "Yeah, that's nice, but I can pick up the phone and talk to any CEO of a company. It's not always what you know, it's who you know and what you've done." That doesn't shut them up, though.

I couldn't have been the easiest father for my girls in terms of dating and dances, that kind of stuff. There was some function one year, and my daughter was going with this boy. I told her to tell that kid to bring his ass over to my house, that I need to talk with him beforehand. The day of the dance, the kid comes and knocks on the door. He's standing there, all smiles, has his little boutonniere on his tuxedo, etc. He's looking good. This dude is ready.

Then I open the door. Before he could open his mouth, I said, "What part of 'bring your ass over here so I could talk to you before you take my daughter out' did you not understand? Do we have a listening problem?" The boy is standing there looking at me like I'm crazy. He was shaking with fear.

Then I hear someone laughing behind him down the walk, and it was his mother. She was laughing so hard. Then Karen heard them and she runs down the stairs. The mothers knew each other. It's all well and good, and they are about to leave. I stopped the young man and said, "Let me tell you something. I sprinkled baby powder all over my daughter. If she comes home with one fingerprint, you're going to see me again, and this time I'm not going to be so nice."

My daughter said he took her to the event, opened and closed the door at the entrance for her…and she didn't see him for the rest of the night. That was the last time any of my kids went on a one-on-one thing. After that my girls did group dating, where all of their friends would go together.

I told my girls about how I read this study that said 98 percent of relationships in high school don't go anywhere. Why the hell would you lose your virginity for something like that? Even in college 86 percent of relationships break up, don't end in marriage. I gave them that information and let them figure it out. I did all I could and told them, "You're on your own now. You're on your own." Karen and I can't always be there for them. You just hope they make the right decisions. If they need me, I'm always a call away.

My girls got a lot of tough love from me because I always figured my son could fight his own battles just like I did. I was always hard on the girls, though, a little bit extra hard on them, for whatever reason. Here's something else I always tell each of my daughters: if she has a boyfriend, or someday a husband, and he puts his hands on her, don't worry about calling the cops or anything else. Just give me a call, and I promise you I'll take care of that situation. That's not going to end well. No, sir. That's not going to end well if someone puts his hands on one of my daughters.

Really, the overwhelming majority of my life has been about the three F's: family, football, and faith. Without any of those three, I wouldn't still be alive. I am convinced of that.

Religion is ritual. I'm not a ritual guy. I'm a spiritual guy. I believe that the word of God moves us. When you go to church, you have the Bible interpreted for you, but I believe God wrote the Bible in a way that we can take our own wisdom from the readings. Sometimes I get frustrated when I attend church because they start talking about what this word in Latin represents, and then it throws off what I think the passage means. I also don't like when political stuff is mentioned during church. My life is reading his word directly from his book, though I do listen to sermons a lot, more so on tape, on my phone, YouTube, etc.

I know my mother has been frustrated with me because we didn't have a family church when my kids were growing up like we did back in Virginia. Still, my kids grew up knowing who Jesus Christ is. And to this day, I send them a text message every morning with an inspirational Bible verse. That's the best I can do for them. They know where I stand with God, and that's the only thing that matters to me.

If you have that seed rooted in you, like my mother did for me, you're going to come back to the word because God always allows us to come home again. I failed a whole bunch of times in many different ways, but every time I failed, I dropped to my knees and God prospered me threefold.

God has always been very important in my life. He's saved me a lot. There were many nights after I retired when I was in the worst of places, ready to take my own life, and the lone reason I didn't was because of him. I needed to make sure I could always have a relationship with him. I read the Book of Psalms a lot, where they talk about King David, talk about all the hardships he had to go through just to become king. He had all these people, all these stumbling blocks in front of him and he overcame them and became God's own heart. The trials and tribulations that he went through were incredibly inspiring. Then Job, he was a man of conviction. God allowed the devil to take everything from him, even his health, and he still overcame. Jesus was humble, and I think he keeps us all humble. I read the word. I read the Bible from cover to cover about three times a year every year. I can't always quote the Bible verbatim, but once somebody starts a passage, I can usually finish it.

Who I became as a football player, that foundation, really the entire process, was through God. When I was younger, when other kids and my brothers would bully me, when I was slow and chubby, and when I was struggling to read and write, I asked God to give me a talent, to give me one thing at which I was good. And then I started growing and working hard, and that singular talent became football. When I was running hills at James Madison, I would talk to God. I would say, "This is going to make me stronger. The pain and suffering is my price for success." I would do crab exercises up and down that field until I passed out. And I would come to and start crabbing again. Then I would run the stands.

I ran and ran and ran. It wasn't about lifting weights and strength for me. It doesn't matter how strong you are, it's about endurance. It's about who can last until the end. A lot of guys are running around like crazy during the first possession, the first quarter, and then they're done. They're gassed by halftime. I was coming at you 100 percent for 100 plays. Yeah, you might block me 95 times, but those other five plays can change the outcome of a ballgame—a sack, a forced fumble, a big hit, stopping a running back on third and 1.

In order to be great, I would go to practice and then I would come home and I would run. I would have my wife drive the car behind me while I ran at night. Greatness doesn't rest. If you want to achieve greatness, you can't stop. Bill Walsh told me once, "Either you're climbing the mountain or you're going down. You can never stay the same. You're either going up or you're going down." That is the best advice I've ever heard. Preparation, sacrifice, and the willingness to do what it takes—that's the secret to success right there. I was mad at my father growing up because he worked two jobs, but I didn't realize he had to sacrifice family life to put food on the table.

There were many times when I was out there two hours after practice all by myself, running and working, talking to God about what I wanted to do with my life. I wanted a way out of Gladys and poverty. I was convinced that God wanted me to get better, wanted me to be a star.

I tried to take any negative and turn it into a positive. If I had a bad game or made a bad play, I would say, "Let this be a lesson." Even today when I'm doing business, if the deal doesn't happen, I tell God, "This was a great learning experience."

I'm not one of those people who blames God for everything that goes wrong. He has a direction for all of us. And it's not about successes or failures. It's about opportunity. What are you going to do with each opportunity presented in your life? I was given an opportunity to attend college and play football. I didn't deserve that opportunity. I didn't have the grades, I needed to take that SAT like five times, but the opportunity was given to me and I took advantage. I was given a chance to play in the NFL and I made the most of it. I maximized my opportunities. Life is about taking advantage of those opportunities.

My opportunities now are about helping others, whether it be kids, NFL players, or everyone in between. I'm willing to talk with anyone and everyone. And I don't mind sticking my head in a hornet's nest because if I can save one guy, I'm happy with that. I think I've already helped a lot of people with my story.

Throughout my career, guys were telling me that I needed to change, that I needed help. I did not listen. That has haunted me every day since. I'm talking my closest friends, too. Ronnie Lott, who is my best friend, told me I needed help, but I didn't listen. Keena Turner, Michael Carter, those few teammates who I honestly trusted, said the same thing, and I would not listen to anyone. I wouldn't even listen to my own wife. I thought the world was against me, which is how those who are dealing with mental illness feel. Instead of dealing with our own problems, dealing with all the pain, the hurt, the anger, the disappointment that lives inside of us, we project it onto someone else. That's the hardest part to understand.

I love words. I'm fascinated by people who can move nations with their words. I receive a lot of gratification through words. I look for the little things when I'm reading the Psalms. David says, "Though I walk through the valley of the shadow of death, I will fear no evil." I look at David, and everyone was out to kill him. He's going through that valley, he knows people all around him are ready to kill him, but yet he didn't have any fear. He didn't have any anger.

When I played, I tried to emulate Shaka Zulu, the African king. I would watch that 1986 TV miniseries all the time. I think it came out during my rookie year. That one heartbeat when they would all beat that shield, put themselves into a trance, and then jog 30 or 40 miles and fight, that's kind of what King David did.

* * *

My life today is beautiful. I do a lot of charity work. That takes up most of my time. I co-founded Tackle Tomorrow, and we work with Istation, which tries to bring computers and the Internet to low-economic areas. The focus is preschool through third grade because the research says if a kid can't read by the third grade, then they likely won't learn, so we're attacking that age group right now. It's rewarding to me. Every day is a gift to see a kid learning something. I give them the truth, too. Whether it's a kid or a grown man, I try to not only give them my help, but also deal with them honestly. I've fought all of these battles, and let me promise you, 80 percent of them didn't need to be fought. That's a big part of my message right there.

I love being involved. You get to watch the people, you get to dive in with your own hands. I don't just give money. I give time and effort. I let people know I'm there for them. I'm willing to get dirty, not just buy them some material thing and disappear. You let these people in your charity or organization, let them know you love them, that you want to change their world, and then you hope and pray it has a trickle-down effect. They see your love and passion and they become rejuvenated. As long as I'm healthy enough to help those in need, that's my life focus. It's charity work with kids and it's being a vital part in these young men's lives playing football. I let them know you have a friend in me.

I think that's how the NFL has to work. The former players have to be proactive and mentor these young guys. Any time I hear about a player dealing with substance abuse or mental illness, I'm on the phone or I'm driving to his practice. I tell these guys all the time, "Look, I didn't play well with others, but when I was making all that money, my family came first." I wasn't paying bills for anyone besides my family. A lot of these players today, athletes in general, they don't feel like a man unless they have six people around them or they are carrying a gun. They live in fear. One of the reasons I stayed out of trouble during my career was that I stayed home.

When I talk with football players at any level, I tell them the fundamental steps for success. Step one is you have to be in shape. Step two is you must have mental toughness. Step three is you have to be smart by studying that playbook, knowing everyone's role, and watching a lot of film. Step four is you have to possess a skillset, which also means knowing your strengths and your limitations. And step five is you need to have the mind-set to go out there and kick butt.

The difference between a decent player and a great player is a great player has a dog in him. The first guy, somebody hits him, and he's okay with it. But a great player, if he gets hit, he's going to try to hit that person with all of his passion and inner self next time around.

That's the instinct that winners have. There's a Robert Frost quote that I think about often, "The best way out is always through." Later in his life, when asked about what he had learned, Frost said, "In three words I can sum up everything I've learned about life: it goes on."

I love myself for the first time because I'm not afraid. I don't let anyone steal my joy. I'm an open book, where there are no secrets. That's the price I'm willing to pay so that my failures can become someone else's strength. Then maybe they don't have to go through the pain and suffering that I endured.

If I had my choice in how I will be remembered, I guess it would be as a country boy who was tired of living poor, was given an opportunity, and took advantage of it. I've done a lot of great things as a football player, but at the end of the day, it's about what I do now off the field, how I try to inspire not only children, but also NFL players on mental health and life skills in general. I tell them, "I grew up segregated and prejudiced. I was an angry black man who hated the world." They look at me and say, "Wow, who helped you? How did you change?"

And that's where I can help. I have those answers, I've made the changes. I am bipolar. I take my medication. It's not a stigma anymore; it's the truth. Because I have accepted that truth, I can live my life as a free man, free of the torment that raged within my head. Let's be real honest here, I'm not trying to act like an angel when I'm clearly not. I'm just a man who has struggled with his own inner demons and emerged a better man. And now I want to help anyone and everyone I can. That's not a bad legacy right there. That would make for a life I would be pretty proud of living. And I'm doing my best to live that life every day.

Acknowledgments

CHARLES HALEY

I actually wrote another book almost 20 years ago. That one was called *All the Rage*, and at the time, I was filled with more rage than any man should ever experience. I was angry at the world. And honestly, I don't remember much about working on it. Before the interviews with the guy who co-wrote the book, I'd get drunk.

My world has changed in many ways since then. I'm happy. For the first time in my life, I like the man I have become. It was quite the struggle, though. After my playing career, there were the lowest of the lows before finding peace. That's my story, that's the message, that's my objective for writing this book. It's to start a conversation about mental illness. It's to address and inform as many people as I can about how mental illness almost destroyed me and how I can help them to overcome the demons I faced.

I saw this sign not long ago that made a lot of sense to me: the three Cs of life are choices, chances, and changes. Then it read: "You must make a Choice to take a Chance or your life will never Change."

I have been fortunate to be surrounded by a lot of love and support through my life, even if I didn't always realize it, and I have many people to thank.

To my kids, Princess, Charles Jr., Brianna, and Madison, my deepest appreciation for always loving me, even though I was so unpredictable, even though the light may have been dark, I hope my love always shined through. I tell them all the time that greatness is not born but made, and that greatness shows its head daily.

I also want to thank their mother, my ex-wife Karen, who will always hold a special place in my heart. So much of this journey would have been impossible without her guidance and support. I still and always will love her.

To Coach Mac (Challace McMillin), thanks for believing in me as I believed in you. Also Danny Wilmer for recruiting me. Both men made it clear from my first day at James Madison that education would come before football. And Bill Walsh, thank you for always being there for me, I love you like a father.

I was blessed with a ton of great coaches: Tommy Hart, Jimmy Johnson, Barry Switzer, Butch Davis, and George Seifert. I really owe George so much. He explained to me everyone's role on the defense and truly made me a great player because of the wisdom he shared. I am grateful that we are on friendly terms; he's a wonderful man.

My mother and father, Virginia and George Sr., thank you for your love and being patient with me, for holding my hand when others abandoned me. Also my brothers, George Jr., James, David, and Lawrence.

My gratitude to my professional-type friends who helped me get through the tough times and keep me on track: Al Merchant, Monique Thompson, Dr. Wiggin, and Dr. Urschel. Also my friends at my 7:30 group, they are like brothers for teaching me how to become confident in my skills and help me get over my past.

To coach Bill McPherson with the 49ers, thank you for teaching me to be a professional and how to study film.

To the best owners in all of sports, Jerry Jones and Eddie DeBartolo Jr. It's ridiculous I was able to play for both of these great men.

All my defensive line mates, thanks for being my rock. The love and respect we have for each other will never end. My teammates: Dwaine Board, Michael Carter, Don Griffin, Ronnie Lott, Guy McIntyre, Jerry Rice, Larry Roberts, and Keena Turner with the 49ers and Troy Aikman, Tony Casillas, Chad Hennings, Michael Irvin, Russell Maryland, Emmitt Smith, Big Nate Newton, Larry Allen, and Tony Tolbert with the Cowboys. Thank you for your friendship and loyalty.

I also want to say thanks to the team doctors over the years and the equipment men who worked so hard and made my life easier.

Also good friends Bob Bowie, who has given me purpose; Andrew Alvarado; and Jaime Najera. Lane and Hank Wendorf, guys who love me and the man I have become. I'll always have your back. Brett Lindig and Brent Chesney, thank you both for opening up your home and letting me be part of your family. And no one could have had better in-laws than Salis and Carrie Smith. Rest in peace.

Andrew and Jaime, thanks for making me go to the dual diagnosis in Tennessee that turned my life around. That's where I got the big results I needed so badly. I love you two meatheads. You turned my life around.

To one of my best friends, Alfred McGeachy, and my godson, Donovan.

Unfortunately, through the years I have forgotten their names, but to all the tutors and those wonderful women in the reading and writing centers at James Madison. There is no way for me to thank you for inspiring me to stay with it and keep working. The road to success was very hard, but the reward—a college education—was even bigger.

I'd also like to thank all the writers who elected me to the greatest honor of my life and the great people at the Pro Football Hall of Fame. My eternal appreciation.

Life is difficult but becomes easier with the kindness of others, and Carol Roberts has shown her support, friendship, and love when times have been good and bad. She's pulled me from the darkness time and again, and business-wise, she's been my rock. I can't thank her enough.

I also want to thank the people at Tackle Tomorrow, my charitable foundation. And to all the players who I work with and try to help, remember one thing: you do not have to go through anything alone. I'm always here.

JEFF SULLIVAN

When Tom Bast of Triumph Books called me about writing a book with Charles Haley, my first thought was this could be utterly fantastic—one of the coolest experiences of my career—or he's going to kick my ass before a single word is written.

It was the former. And then some. Sure, there were some good-natured (I think) threats, but Charles couldn't have been better to work with. There are many stories about the five months we spent on this project, my favorite being a random phone call on a Friday morning in December when my wife and I were in Washington, D.C. In the midst of talking about his parents, he said, "I've always been fascinated by those rare leaders who have the masses follow them and change the world, be it Jesus Christ, George Washington, Alexander the Great, Churchill, even the horrible ones like Hitler. And of course Dr. Martin Luther King."

Charles asked me if I was going to see the MLK Memorial while we were in the city, and I said we were that very day. He started reciting some of the 14 MLK quotes that are on the Inscription Wall on either side of the memorial. Later that morning I played the recording of our conversation back as I stood there, staring at the quotes, and Charles knew them verbatim. The man kept finding ways to impress me with his intelligence and sincerity.

Several references helped in research for this book, including ESPN.com, Pro-Football-Reference.com, DallasCowboys.com, *All the Rage*, and *The Dallas Morning News*.

From Triumph, I'd like to thank publisher Mitch Rogatz, my superb (and patient) editor Jeff Fedotin, and Tom Bast.

This book is infinitely better because of the efforts of my good friends, Kurt Daniels and Barnaby Hall, and my wife, Danielle. My thanks to Ronnie Lott and Jerry Jones for their heartfelt efforts on two world-class forewords. And to Rich Dalrymple with the Cowboys for his assistance.